An Altitude SuperGuide

D0752650

Totem Poles

An Altitude SuperGuide

TOTEM POLES

by Pat Kramer

Altitude Publishing Canada Ltd.
Canadian Rockies/Vancouver

Totem poles come from the creative expression of people

Acknowledgements

Sincere thanks are due to the many native people across British Columbia who helped to give this book its shape. Many took time to give directions and make suggestions. Others kindly shared their traditions and ceremonies. Still others prepared many a barbecue salmon feast. To the native dancers, artists, carvers, friends and passers-by who allowed me to photograph them, and to those who for one reason or another do not appear here, an expression of appreciation. To those of my adult students at the Native Education Centre who acted as my inspiration; to all those who gave me permission to intrude with my camera; to those gracious elders who were kind, (though my time has been all too short); to my native friends who smiled and gently corrected me; and to my native grandfather who took me travelling at an early age, I express my gratitude. A sampling of these fine people and their children appears on the page opposite.

From these fine folks I bring a message. When asked what they would most like to see in contemporary writings, many wish to send one clear message. First People are not trapped in the past; they are not living in 1750 or 1850 or 1950. And though they have endured great hardship, they did not perish. Today, they are alive and well. It is true they are part of an animated tradition with strong roots in the past. However, tradition is not static. Those of the present are reshaping their lives (as they always have) for the benefit of future generations. While respecting the past, the present generation carries on, always adapting, always innovating, always improving their ways. This is the way all vibrant societies thrive.

Message received, and message delivered.

There are others to whom we owe recognition but whose names are not recorded. Spiraling back in time are countless but nameless master carvers and their apprentices who inspired the carvers of the present. Though their names may be obscured with the passing of the seasons, their work breathes through their successors to the present moment.

To the two little Coast Salish girls whose photo appears here but whose guardians thought should remain unnamed, here is the fulfillment of a promise. One fine summer afternoon at the War Canoe Races, these two sparkling youngsters heard I was doing a book about Totem Poles. After circling around a bit, they shyly implied that they might like to appear in this book. "But you are not totem poles!" my adult wit gently teased them. "Oh yes, we make a very fine totem pole," they insisted. So here you are. I have kept my word. Now the book is complete and no finer totem pole can be found within these pages. For the best "totem" of all is the creative enthusiasm of a new generation.

Publication Information

Altitude Publishing Canada Ltd.
1500 Railway Avenue
Canmore, Alberta T1W 1P6

Copyright 1998, 1999 © Pat Kramer
Base Maps Copyright 1994 © Magellan Geographix

10 9 8 7 6 5 4

Extreme care has been taken to ensure that all information presented in this book is accurate and up-to-date, and neither the author nor the publisher can be held responsible for any errors.

Canadian Cataloguing in Publication Data

Kramer, Pat
Totem Poles

(An Altitude SuperGuide)
Includes bibliographical references and index.
ISBN 1-55153-629-3

1. Totem poles--British Columbia--History.
1. Title. II. Series.
E98.T65K72 1998   731'.7   C98-910385-4

Made in Western Canada

Printed and bound in Canada
by Friesen Printers, Altona, Manitoba.

Altitude GreenTree Program

Altitude Publishing will plant twice as many trees as were used in the manufacturing of this product.

Front cover photo: Full face image

Frontispiece: Painted totem pole

Back cover photo: Thunderbird

Pages 4 and 5: Thunderbird watching over modern day Vancouver

Project Development

Concept/Art Direction	Stephen Hutchings
Design	Stephen Hutchings, Sandra Davis
Editor	Anne Norman
Maps	Sandra Davis
Scanning	Debra Symes
Electronic Page Layout	Sandra Davis
Financial Management	Laurie Smith
Index/proofreading	Alison Barr

We acknowledge the financial support of the Government of Canada through the Book Publishing Industry Development Program (BPIDP) for our publishing activities.

A Note from the Publisher

The world described in Altitude SuperGuides is a unique and fascinating place. It is a world filled with surprise and discovery, beauty and enjoyment, questions and answers. It is a world of people, cities, landscape, animals and wilderness as seen through the eyes of those who live in, work with, and care for this world. The process of describing this world is also a means of defining ourselves.

It is also a world of relationship, where people derive their meaning from a deep and abiding contact with the land–as well as from each other. And it is this sense of relationship that guides all of us at Altitude to ensure that these places continue to survive and evolve in the decades ahead.

Altitude SuperGuides are books intended to be used, as much as read. Like the world they describe, *Altitude SuperGuides* are evolving, adapting and growing. Please write to us with your comments and observations, and we will do our best to incorporate your ideas into future editions of these books.

Stephen Hutchings
Publisher

visit Altitude's web site:
www.altitudepublishing.com

Contents

The **Totem SuperGuide** is organized according to the following colour scheme:

The Origin and History of Totem Poles ....
Totem Pole Symbols and Ceremonies ....
Identifying Totem Figures..............................
Land of the Totem Poles................................
Recommended Reading and Index ....

1. The Origin and History of Totem Poles

Skidegate in Haida Gwaii in 1878 was a thriving village at the apex of the Golden Age of totem poles. Dr. George M. Dawson, the photographer, and James Deans, a contemporary researcher, note that Haida clan status was partially indicated by the height of one's pole. All poles shown here were taken down at the behest of missionaries about a decade later.

Long, long ago, obscured by the passage of time, people living along the Pacific Coast of North America developed a culture based on the abundance surrounding them. Tidal pools yielded hoards of shellfish. Rivers were laden with migrating salmon. The air was filled with flocks of waterfowl. Forests soared with mighty trees. To survive and thrive in this environment, nameless individuals painstakingly invented tools, refined their techniques, and passed on their knowledge. In turn, their expertise in the technology of survival freed up the leisure time required to establish a rich and vibrant cultural life. Long-ago artisans turned to the decorative potential of stone and wood, particularly cedar. Excavated tools suggest that coastal people were working with wood by about 5000 BC. The embodiment of eons of artistic traditions can be seen today, woven into the fascinating aboriginal art and totem poles of the First Nations of the region known as the Northwest Coast.

Early Art and Objects

Anthropologists estimate that cultural patterns based on wealth and leisure time permit certain individuals to specialize at least part-time in the arts. Along the Northwest Coast, these patterns were well established by 3500 BC. Because wooden objects disintegrate over time, stone carvings and various tools are the only

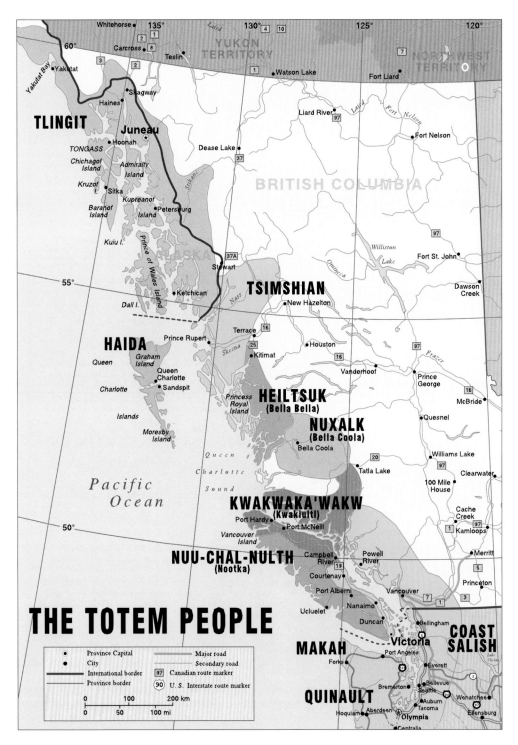

THE TOTEM PEOPLE

TLINGIT

HAIDA

TSIMSHIAN

HEILTSUK
(Bella Bella)

NUXALK
(Bella Coola)

KWAKWAKA'WAKW
(Kwakiutl)

NUU-CHAL-NULTH
(Nootka)

MAKAH

QUINAULT

COAST SALISH

YUKON TERRITORY

NORTHWEST TERRITORY

BRITISH COLUMBIA

ALASKA

Pacific Ocean

Queen Charlotte Sound

Whitehorse • 135°
Carcross •
Teslin •
3
Yakutat • Yakutat Bay
Skagway •
Haines •
TONGASS
Juneau ★
Hoonah •
Chichagof Island
Admiralty Island
Kruzof I.
Sitka •
Kupreanof Island
Baranof Island
Petersburg •
Kuiu I.
Prince of Wales Island
Dall I.
Ketchican •
Stewart
Prince Rupert •
Graham Island
Queen
Charlotte
Queen Charlotte • Sandspit
Charlotte
Princess Royal Island
Islands
Moresby Island

130° 4 10
Laird
1
Watson Lake • Fort Liard
Liard River • 97
Laird
Fort Nelson
Dease Lake •
37
Stikine
Nass
37A
New Hazelton •
Terrace • 16
Skeena
25
Kitimat •
Houston •
Vanderhoof •
Bella Coola •
Tatla Lake • 20
Port Hardy •
Port McNeill •
Vancouver Island
Campbell River • 19
Courtenay •
Port Alberni •
Ucluelet •
Nanaimo •
Duncan •
Powell River
Vancouver
Port Angeles •
Forks •
Bremerton •
Hoquiam •
Aberdeen •
Olympia ★
Centralia •

125°
7
Fort Liard
Fort Nelson •
Williston Lake
Omineca
Fort St. John •
Dawson Creek
97
Fraser
Prince George •
McBride •
Quesnel •
Williams Lake •
97
Clearwater •
100 Mile House
Cache Creek
1
Kamloops •
Merritt •
5
Princeton •
7
3
1
Bellingham •
Victoria ★
Everett •
Bellevue
Seattle •
Auburn
Tacoma
Wenatchee •
Ellensburg •

120°
NORTHWEST TERRITORY
60°
55°
50°

The art of Northwest Coast Natives is eons old. Only the medium has changed over the centuries. This modern totem figure, said to be the first man to discover the earth, is hauntingly similar to an ancient petroglyph located deep in the forest near Bella Coola, BC.

jects; bone implements; chisels; sharp blades of nephrite; and well-decorated baskets, canoe paddles, and wooden storage boxes.

Other community sites excavated along the coast of present-day British Columbia, dating from AD 500 to 1200, have revealed carved combs, crafted charms and amulets, rounded human-figure stone bowls, and bone pins decorated with animal and human heads. All these objects show proficient stone and woodworking skills. Even a paint pallet was recovered. Though no totem poles or wooden totem figures are known from this period, small decorative objects in everyday use show a highly developed symbol system. The figure of Wolf shows up in one beautifully carved comb (ca. AD 800), as does Raven (ca. 1000 BC) and a number of unidentified large-eyed creatures (ca. AD 1000). Though our curiosity is great, researchers can only guess broadly what these creatures meant in their own time.

Rock Art Sites

Over 600 rock art sites are presently known along the Northwest Coast from southwestern Alaska through British Columbia to the lower Columbia River and extending into California. The sites are thought to date from 4500 BC to about AD 1800.

Researchers continue to explore the shapes found in these once-hidden areas and many surmise that they were the work of shamans and their initiates. Young people were introduced to the spiritual side of life through a process of

objects that remain to suggest these patterns. At one site dated to about 1000 BC, researchers uncovered a number of small art objects in everyday use. Another site, dated to 500 BC, yielded copper bracelets, decorated warrior weapons, slate and bone amulets, stone labrets (for pierced lips), sea otter teeth made into mosaics, and handles on chisels decorated with

human faces. One rare site, completely underwater, fortuitously preserved ancient wooden and organic objects in an anaerobic environment. Dated to about AD 500, this rich find suggests that the potlatch tradition was well underway and the status of upper-class families already symbolized by heraldic crests. Recovered objects include mauls; antler wedges; small art ob-

Though this photograph was taken in the early 1900s, it shows old-style mortuary figures of the type reported by the first trading ships mapping the coast. These types of carvings predate contact.

vision questing. Sequestered deep within the forest, the fasting initiates first found their "song"—two or three sentences with deep meaning. Eventually, they spoke with animals who changed their lives. The art found along cliffs and ocean shorelines may be either laborious attempts to contact a spirit-animal or a permanent record of the encounter after it occurred.

Rock art sites are decorated with red ochre paintings and known as pictographs, or they are abraded with sharp tools and known as petroglyphs. Though the curvilinear styles are recognizable and the creatures seem linked by some type of mythological framework, researchers can only guess at their exact meaning.

The art forms now seen in the totem poles of coastal Native people extend back over the centuries. Shapes have evolved and slowly varied, but the concept of dividing flat spaces with incised lines and characteristic curved shapes was widely practised from the dawn of civilization. The art of today has never deviated from the roots that make it recognizable as an art form belonging entirely to the First People of the Northwest Coast.

Life before Contact

By AD 1000 and up to the point of contact with Europeans around 1740, Northwest Coast artifacts show that Winter Dance mask ceremonies were a well-established part of life. Various bands of people lived in villages of plank longhouses during the winter, then spread out in summer to work in berry-picking grounds or to

fish in fertile salmon migration areas. Climatic conditions were fairly stable.

At this time, bands developed a workable three-tiered class system. The upper classes lived a privileged life with the obligation to accumulate wealth and then give it all away in an elaborate ceremony known as a potlatch. The middle classes were artisans, cooks, hunters, gatherers, and workers who could rate extra privileges if their artistic works were particularly admired. The underclass were slaves, captured during raids against neighbouring bands. Their very lives depended on the whim of their upper-class owners.

The objects recovered from this period are highly decorated and show that talented members of the band were

John Webber, the artist on Captain Cook's third expedition, drew this rendering of a Nootka longhouse in 1778. This is the first time an academic outsider provided visual evidence of carved or painted poles.

employed full-time to render ceremonial art. Women and men spun and wove mountain goat fleece into blankets. Other pieces of clothing were woven from cedar bark. Watertight bentwood boxes were used for cooking and storage. A shaman's "crown" was made of grizzly bear claws. Chiefs wore carved headdresses with ermine tails. Food dishes were carved into representational shapes. Chiefs owned decorated canes known as talking sticks.

Between 1500 and 1700, several coastal bands incised designs on the interior posts of their large post-and-beam plankhouses. Because of the nature of their nephrite and obsidian tool blades, however, most carved objects were relatively small. The Haida report that special "logs" washed up on their shores during this period and from these they recovered iron. At first contact, several coastal bands already fashioned iron tools. Researchers surmise that these "logs" were masts that floated in from far-away shipwrecks.

It takes strong, durable tools to carve large wooden objects with speed and efficiency. With the few iron tools they owned, long before the arrival of Europeans, some bands were already carving freestanding human-sized wooden mortuary (memorial) figures. The ancient practice of carving of human-sized wooden or stone figures is a characteristic that Northwest Coast Natives share with both the aboriginals of Hawaii and the Maoris of New Zealand, although no academic studies link these peoples or their traditions.

Sporadic First Russian Contacts: 1740 to 1780

Around 1738, Russian ships and traders arrived along the Northwest Coast and began an active industry in sea otter pelts. In 1741, Captain Vitus Bering landed for six hours at Cape St. Elias, Alaska. He observed carved interior house posts. Whether these carvings resembled modern totem poles is not known. At that time, any totemic or family crest activity was the privilege of the upper classes and therefore would be considered a secret and private matter.

Illustrating the class system, a box held aloft by obedient slaves once contained the remains of an upper-class person.

The Sea Otter Trade: 1774 to 1830

Many Europeans visited the region to take advantage of the sea otter trade. In 1774, explorer Juan Pérez of Spain sailed along the coast as far north as Haida Gwaii (the Queen Charlotte Islands) but the weather kept him from landing. Later, Spanish mariners traded in sea otter pelts and enjoyed a lively commerce in copper. As copper was an important component in potlatches, additional Spanish supplies were welcomed.

About 1778, the British began a succession of voyages along the coast. A scientific expedition under the direction of Captain James Cook rested for repairs for three weeks at Nootka Sound on present-day Vancouver Island. Their careful records mention monstrous masks, wooden chests, and ceremonial objects decorated in an elaborate style. They also report carved and painted interior house posts and painted house fronts, but there is no mention of freestanding totem poles. John Webber, the ship's artist on Cook's third and final voyage, painted several renditions of Nootka longhouses. One illustration (page 15) depicts some sort of faces on two interior house posts. His 1778 drawing is the earliest known academic documentation of decorated poles.

An elder holds a talking stick while a totem carver "cleanses" the group with a cedar bough. Talking sticks dated to AD 1000 have been recovered.

The Concept of Transformation

THE CHANGING OF animals and supernatural creatures into other forms or humans, as well as the occasional transformation of humans into animals, is an important component of totem pole stories. Transformation is accomplished without effort and is sometimes referred to as shape shifting. Characterized as "taking off" or "putting on" a skin coat, transformation can be accomplished without a trace of the former creature in evidence.

While in its altered form, the transformed creature may seduce another, win a combat, receive gifts or food, or effect a revenge. Some creatures transform in order to attend human dance ceremonies or to hold their own; a few do it to look in on or assist humans. Trickster figures like Raven are particularly adept at changeovers and in addition to becoming living incarnations, they can manifest as wooden dishes, dirt, pine needles, or totem poles. On Northwest Coast totem poles, transforming figures are carved with large horizontal lips, animal or partially human heads, and partially human bodies. Characteristically, the back, human-shaped legs remain in the haunch position of the animal.

Mosquito

By contrast Webber shows Nootka house exteriors of the day as unornamented.

American, British, French, Spanish, and Italian ships all actively plied the waters along North America's Pacific coast during the heyday of the sea otter trade. Though many forays arrived between 1780 and 1830, these naval traders did not always venture into the villages. Many preferred to remain on board, trading from the quiet security of their ships. However, the trade process had an effect on the Native communities. With the sudden increase in wealth and goods, and an abundance of new metal tools, tradition dictated a corresponding need for the upper classes to mount potlatch feasts. Each chief strained to outdo his rivals in terms of grandeur, honours, memorials, remembrances, and ceremonials. Researchers speculate that totem poles, as they are known today, evolved during this period.

In 1786, the La Pérouse expedition visited the Tlingit people at Lituya Bay, Alaska. Though they travelled with an artist, there is no mention of totem poles. In 1787 Captain George Dixon visited the Native people at Yakutat Bay, Alaska, and Haida Gwaii, BC. Though his artist recorded details of native spoons and trays, there is no mention of totem poles. However, only a few years later, in 1791, Spanish artist José Cardero, a member of the Italian Malaspina expedition, made drawings of several mortuary figures in the same village. Potlatch feasts of the day included the carving and dedication of memorials. This might explain the sudden appearance of the figures.

Techniques in handling large logs rapidly improved with the introduction of iron. Native people used new metal parts to fashion tools such as the axe, adze, and curved knife following the form of their earlier implements. Their art forms, story figures, and heraldic crest traditions were already many centuries old and well developed. The new tools were used to produce traditional art forms on a larger scale.

John Jewitt, a sailor captured in 1788, was forced into slavery by the Nootka people. He later escaped, and in 1791 wrote a book—a best-seller in Europe. His writings talk of "great wooden images" on Graham Island and of "large trees carved and painted." John Barlett, artist aboard the *Gustavus* in 1791, made the first rough pen drawing of an outdoor heraldic pole. It is a house support in front of a Haida longhouse. This adds the second academic bit of visual information showing that house front poles were under

Serving much like a monarch's sceptre, a carved "talking stick" is about one metre (3 feet) tall. To bring a group to order, an elder pounds it on the floor. Some believe these decorated staffs may be the precursors of full-sized totem poles.

construction among the Haida people.

Clearly, widespread pot-latching activity was afoot. Since iron tools made wood carving simpler and faster and since newfound wealth made necessary the giving of pot-latches, the beams of long-houses began to show more decoration both inside and outside, new forms of carvings were produced, and new sur-names, new ceremonials, and new crests were sanctified. However, the right to give a potlatch and to own heraldic crests remained firmly in the hands of a few upper-class el-ders.

Meanwhile, in 1793, Alexander Mackenzie arrived on the Pacific coast. Having made the first overland trek across Canada on foot and by canoe (a decade before the famed Lewis and Clark expedi-tion), his report on inland Na-tives makes no mention of totem poles among the Bella Coola people. He did however report that some people deco-rated their interior house posts. Mackenzie was quite surprised by the number of iron pots and tools the Natives owned. In 1792, only one year earlier, along the coast by way of Cape Horn, Captain George Vancouver reported many gi-gantic wooden human mortu-ary statues. That same year, Etienne Marchand, leading a French sailing expedition, re-ported "paintings everywhere, everywhere sculpture, among a nation of hunters." He also reported that "every man is a painter or a sculptor." In 1794, resourceful US Captain Roberts of the *Jefferson* com-manded his own carpenters

Argillite is only found on the Haida Gwaii. Made from a soft slate first quarried openly in the 1820s, these small carvings are close in size to traditional arts, and quickly became valued collectibles.

and crew to plane, paint, and erect a freestanding imitation "totem pole" of their own on the tip of Dall Island. Though they erected the structure to aid in their trade negotiations, there is no written report of the Haida's reaction to the first non-native simulated pole. In 1799, American William Stur-gis visited the Haida in the ves-sel *Eliza*. He reported the Haida's love of ornamentation in every aspect of their life, from their personal clothing to elaborately painted designs, inside and outside their long-houses. He makes no mention of interior or exterior totem poles, leading academics to speculate that while tall poles did exist, they were still not common in all the villages.

By 1800, mortuary carvings were being consistently re-ported, not only in Haida Gwaii, but sporadically for 1500 kilometres (950 miles) up and down the west coast. Fur-thermore, the carvings seemed to be more numerous and more elaborate with each

passing season. From 1803 to 1805, a Russian expedition un-der the command of Captains Krusenstern and Liansky packed up a significant collec-tion of Tlingit art and removed it to St. Petersburg. It is not known whether these articles survived later Russian up-heavals.

The first documented date known to outsiders involving the formal adoption of totem crests is 1808. A party of inland Gitksan Natives celebrated their recent visit to the new Fort St. James fur-trading post

The first true freestanding totem poles were apparently constructed by the inland Tsimshian, Gitksan, and Nisga'a peoples along the Nass and Skeena Rivers. Sought after and acquired by museum collectors in the late 1800s, many were shipped around the world. A few were saved, restored, or replicated and stand today in and around Kitwanga, BC.

by adopting crests and building a detached totem pole. That particular totem pole featured representations of European breeds of dogs, the fortified fort, and wide wagon roads. Certainly not the Gitsan's first freestanding pole, scholars disagree on when the people of the Skeena and Nass Rivers started building detached poles. Some guess as early as 1775, though by following the path of iron tools, that date could be some decades later.

In 1820, a black soft stone called argillite was discovered (or revealed to the outside world) at Slatechuck Mountain on Haida Gwaii. With the sea otter trade in rapid decline,

the Haida eagerly began to fashion the material into carved pipes, bowls, and small copies of totem poles. Curio dealers, just beginning to discover the beauty of west coast art, snapped up the items from mariners. As soon as argillite items were put up for sale in 1826, a Finnish trader in the service of a Russian-American company assembled a collection and sent it back to Finland. Sadly, the assemblage was later destroyed in a museum fire.

Though the objects were made strictly for sale to outsiders, argillite subjects are based on ancient traditions and are closer to the size and scale of native art before contact. In 1822, artist Ludovic Choris, who had travelled on a 15-year voyage around the world, published, in Paris, a detailed drawing of an intricate Haida argillite Raven tongue-thrusting pipe. His illustration is significant because it is the first to show the intricacy of design so well developed among the people.

From 1830 to 1840, the land-based Hudson's Bay Company (HBC) founded Fort Simpson and replaced the declining sea otter trade with an expanded market for marten, bear, otter, and beaver. Native settlements tended to move and to spring up near trading areas.

This photo, taken at a 1903 potlatch, shows a tradition with very ancient roots. The potlatch host holds aloft a copper—the symbol of his wealth. He will later break the copper and disperse pieces of it among his equals. This practice all but ceased about 1920.

Golden Age of Totem Poles: 1830 to 1895

A period of prolific totem pole carving took place during the mid- to late-1800s among all Northwest Coast Native people, especially the Haida, Tlingit, Tsimshian, Gitksan, Nisga'a, and Kwakiutl. Each evolved an active industry producing their own types of totem poles. During this productive era, carving techniques improved, new traditions solidified, and the written recording of old legends began in earnest. (The stories told in Chapter 3 of this book originate from this period.)

It is difficult to pinpoint which native cultures contributed most to the art of early totem pole carving, but the Haida certainly hold an honoured place. By 1830, many Haida served as sailors

"Low Man on the Totem Pole"

THIS COMMON expression refers to someone or something with lack of rank or status. With real totem poles, however the opposite is true. The lowest figures are often considered the most important. Since they are at eye-level to observers they are carved with great attention to detail. Figures placed on the bottom 2 metres (6 feet) of totems are carefully carved and greatly detailed. All totem poles are carved by a master carver and a team of apprentices. The helpers do the high up parts and the master carver finishes the low end of the pole. Higher-up figures are more representational and, if anything, slightly less important.

Frog peeks out from a Bear

on ships up and down the coast. Learning the art of scrimshaw (engraving whale's teeth) from seasoned sailors, they immediately applied the techniques to carving argillite and producing silver jewellery. The Haida were teachers too. When in port between Alaska and the state of Washington, they visited nearby Native communities. Each village received the benefit of considerable Haida expertise. In spite of periodic outbreaks of smallpox, the Haida also began many projects on their own islands. Their villages became a marvelous mixture of longhouses and totem poles. Some Alaskan villagers even hired Haida people to carve their first village poles. However, the Tlingit were quick studies and never repeated the exercise.

During this period, the ceremonies surrounding the carving and raising of totem poles were formalized. Before this period, a few select elders controlled the carving of clan symbols. After 1840, new procedures were adopted to enable a wider range of upper-class people (including the nouveau riche) to legally own heraldic crest symbols and story figures. New carvers established traditions and devised methods to formally pass their skills on to younger carvers. The potlatch too became more standardized and its practice spread to interior and southern bands having no former potlatch traditions.

Fort Victoria was established about 1843 and the Beaver clan was founded from members of older clans—mainly the Eagle clans who had traded earlier with the Russians and early European expeditions. The Beaver clans are people who have the right to trade in beaver pelts.

Between 1850 and 1880, several feuds erupted over totem pole practices. Phratries (native kinship divisions) argued over who was entitled to the tallest poles and who had the rights to use certain figures. To show subservience to a more powerful chief, certain clans were forced to chop off their poles; others were made to cut off or deface offending crests. The most bitter feud broke out along the Nass River. There, rights to the tallest totem led to pole chopping and a brutal murder.

The Decline of the Golden Age

Several factors entered into the rapid decline and the eventual hiatus of the newly developed art of large totem pole carving. Though pole building continued defiantly after 1900 in certain areas such as Alert Bay, strong forces acted to stop the practice completely in most other locations.

The scourge of smallpox from 1832 onwards, and particularly in 1862, decimated many bands and struck the Haida hard. The population on Haida Gwaii estimated at 7000 in 1835, dwindled to 800 by 1885. Though vaccine was brought in, only 500 were vaccinated before thousands perished. During the epidemic, only one person survived after contracting the disease.

Haida survivors of the smallpox epidemic huddle shyly at the village of Yan. Many once-thriving villages were gradually abandoned after 1862 because there were too few survivors to carry on.

Ninstints, Yan, and several other well-developed Haida villages were abandoned when there were too few survivors to carry on. Among the Kwakiutl people, from an estimated population of 17,000 people at contact, the lowest level of 2370 people was reached in 1898. Of these, only 637 were males. There were over 900 vacant positions in the upper-class nobility system. The scale of devastation from outbreaks of both smallpox and measles can hardly be imagined.

The second factor leading to the eventual cessation of totem pole building was missionary work that began in earnest by the mid-1800s. Though totem poles served as heraldic crests and story figures and were never worshipped, well-meaning missionaries mistook the poles for pagan symbols. Pole building gradually ceased in areas where missionaries were active, and mysterious or deliberate fires swept away existing poles. In several cases in Alaska and along the BC coast, the Natives themselves, in bursts of zeal, chopped and burned their own poles.

In 1833, there were a number of new poles raised in HBC's Fort Simpson; by 1853, there was no trace of them. In 1876 a Christian missionary, Henry Collison, arrived in Haida Gwaii and reported totem poles in front of every house, were "fraught with meaning to the people themselves." He went on to report that a fellow missionary at Fort Simpson, "has induced them to take them all down and de-

Maori Poles

ACCORDING TO MAORI belief, the rubbing of noses signifies the mixing of breath and reinforces the breath of the world.

In New Zealand, Maori wood sculptures are not called totem poles, but they do serve some of the same purposes. The hardwood posts are the likenesses of ancestors who are not to be forgotten. Traditionally, the posts served as a family tree or a record for one's progeny, and the people decorated posts

The Maori of New Zealand produce poles

inside and outside their meeting houses. They also embellished most of their everyday objects.

Swirling patterns were applied to weapons, boxes, canoes, flutes, tools, and houses. Grotesque posts were designed to frighten away enemies. Called the Vikings of the Sunrise, the Maoris are known to have arrived in New Zealand from Hawaii about 1000 years ago. There are no academic studies linking these ancient rovers to the Northwest Coast of North America, but the parallels are interesting.

A burial ground along the Fraser River, photographed in the 1920s, illustrates burial figures of the type that mariners first reported for 1500 kilometres (950 miles) along the northwest coast in the decades just before and after 1800. The cross is a modern addition.

stroy them." Collison went on to take similar actions. First the poles at Skidegate, then those at Old Masset, were taken down.

In 1870 a visiting, educated European called the Haida, Bella Bella, Tsimshian, and Tlingit "nations of artists," but much of their activity had already ceased or was carried out in secret. About 1880, the practices surrounding totem pole carving ceased completely among the Haida people as they committed en masse to Christianity. Fortunately, small-sized argillite carvings were popular with collectors and were tolerated because they were seen as encouraging "industriousness" among the people.

By about 1902, missionaries had also effectively dis-couraged the practices around totem pole carving along the Skeena and Nass Rivers. Among the Gitksan, one lone carver named Illameu contin-ued. Ironically, at the same time that totem pole carving ceased everywhere else, it reached an apex among the Kwakiutl and Nootka people.

An old totem pole lies down to rest near a human grave. Almost as soon as Northwest Coast people began making totem poles in quantity, nineteenth century collectors and museum curators began removing them.

However, by 1910, carving had virtually ceased among them too, with the exception of the community of Alert Bay and other isolated communities. Perched on small islands between Vancouver Island and the mainland or in isolated coastal inlets, these little villages stubbornly continued with their old traditions.

Canadian law also played an active role in the decline of totem pole carving. In 1880, the federal government passed the first Indian Act. It makes no mention of feast giving or totem pole carving. But in 1884, the government, with the encouragement of several anthropologists and missionaries, added the soon-to-be-infamous amendment section 116. It forbade the massive giving of "gifts," with imprisonment or large fines as a penalty. Although section 116 was aimed specifically at ending the practice of potlatches, it also affected pole carving because great numbers of poles were constructed in anticipation of potlatch ceremonies.

Forbidding the potlatch effectively ended much totem

Which Ones Are the Eyes?

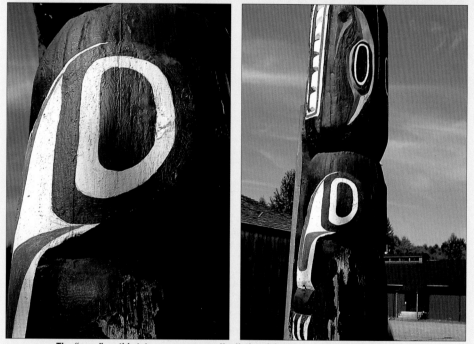

The "eyes" on this totem are more easily distinguished from a distance than up close

ON SOME POLES it is easy to determine the top and bottom of each creature. In other cases, overlapping shapes make it difficult to sort out the beginning of one figure from the ending of another.

Eyes are defined by eyebrows or by eye sockets that are either pinched to a point at both sides or circular and staring ahead.

Eyes are positioned somewhere near mouths. Ovoid shapes, on the other hand, are decorations used to fill spaces. Sometimes the ovoid space filler can be mistaken for an extra eye or a "hidden" creature. Are there extra creatures hidden on totem poles? Generally, there are not.

Illustrated here is Wolf with a long mouth placed vertically. Its eye is surrounded with green. The lower segment is its leg hanging down to its claw. The lower double ovoid is not an additional eye or another creature. Native artists sometimes take an X-ray view of animals and place circular or ovoid designs on joints. In this case the ovoid shows that the shoulder is capable of movement.

An unnamed collector about 1900 strikes a Great White Hunter pose, showing off his acquisition of a rare Chilcotin blanket, a chief's ermine-tail headdress, and a button robe. The removal of native items during the last two decades of the 1800s has been referred to as a collecting rampage.

pole carving. Most bands immediately complied; others ignored the law; a few bands actually increased their holding of potlatches masquerading as "celebrations for the king's coronation" or "Christmas giving to the poor." Many arrests were made. In some cases, plea bargains were arranged. The Native community could sell their regalia and artworks to anthropologists, or their elders could go to jail. In 1885, Bill Uslick of the Pyeachten Reserve at Chilliwack was sentenced to three months in prison for holding a potlatch. Many others were fined in the range of $15—a huge sum at the time. Outsiders consid-

By the 1840s, the Haida were carving traditional designs into silver jewellry. Though the designs are eons old, some of the crosshatching is adapted from scrimshaw techniques the artists learned when working as mariners aboard sailing ships.

ered the potlatch "wasteful" and harmful to the process of assimilation into white society. Most Native communities complied, but Alert Bay near Vancouver Island remained defiant. Continuing in their old ways, the people of Alert

Bay held periodic lavish potlatches. In 1921, Doug Cranmer gave a potlatch so generous that 34 people were charged under section 116. Along with thousands of blankets and food items, he gave away 24 canoes and dozens of sewing machines. Authorities, alarmed at Alert Bay's continuing defiance, came in and seized their extensive potlatch collection of masks and ceremonial objects. Its totem poles were taken soon after. Until 1951, when the law was revoked, potlatches and traditional carving among BC Natives stopped entirely or went underground.

Migration patterns among Native people at this time

also disrupted settled village life and placed additional pressures on long-established customs. In 1887, Alaskan newspapers reported many Natives abandoning their traditional villages for work in salmon-canning factories. While their old villages were left to decay, a few elders proudly erected new poles in front of their houses near the factories. A small renaissance in totem pole building occurred briefly during and after the Klondike Gold Rush of 1897–98. Once again, Native people prospered, and particularly in Alaska and northern British Columbia, there were flurries of potlatches and a number of new poles.

Haida Story: The Origin of Totem Poles

HAIDA PEOPLE SAY that in the time long ago, before white people arrived, a fully carved totem pole once floated ashore. Discovered by the Haida Watchmen, (warriors who defended their island shores) it was a gift from the Creator. From then on, they began to carve large trees in a like manner.

In 1949, this legend assumed larger-than-life propor-tions when a Japanese Ainu pole washed up in Haida Gwaii. Though Japanese poles are far different in appearance, and the roots of Northwest Coast art are well established through archeological digs, this bit of floating evidence led to uninformed speculation that Northwest Coast totem poles were merely "copied."

Museum Acquisition Period: 1870 to 1930

While totem pole construction was in decline in certain areas and actively flourishing in others, ethnographers, museum curators, and anthropologists suddenly discovered the art of the Northwest Coast. Particularly for a 20-year period from 1880 to 1900, collectors combed the region in what has been described as a "collecting

The Tradition Continues

THE EARLIEST TYPE of decorated poles mentioned by European traders were interior house posts. Illustrated first in 1778 by John Webber, artist aboard Captain Cook's ship, they served as stage scenery backdrops. All Winter Dances took place in front of house posts. Most depict common story figures and some were outfitted with hidden pulleys or trapdoors so the players or giant wooden puppets could fly or appear and disappear during the ceremonies.

When families moved to their summer quarters, it was common to take their house planks with them, leaving the posts and supporting beams behind. When families returned, the walls were quickly reassembled.

Shown here are a modern Kwakiutl longhouse with its side walls removed and an archival photograph taken about 1910. These two photographs illustrate that today, Native people research museums and archives to rediscover their old designs, and then replicate them as a continuing link in a very old tradition.

Despite a series of interruptions to the tradition, the present-day totem poles in the Kitwancool area of the Skeena River remain true to their origins.

Hawkwoman attends Winter Dance ceremonies

rampage." At times, the researchers almost scrambled over each other. Hundreds of totem poles and hundreds of thousands of objects were removed and found their way to museums in Washington, DC, Chicago, New York, London, Berlin, Paris, New Zealand, Australia, Ottawa, and Montreal—all far from the Pacific northwest coast. Some of the articles were purchased and removed with permission; others were pilfered or extorted. Some of the academic travellers and acquisitors who moved through the area included Marius Barbeau, Franz Boas, George M. Dawson, Wilson Duff, George T. Emmons, Charles Hill-Tout, Captain Ja-

cobsen, Dr. W.H. Kreiger, Charles and William Newcombe, Alex Rasmussen, Edward Sapir, Harlin I. Smith, James G. Swan, John R. Swanton, and Oliver Wells. Captain Jacobsen alone boasted that he acquired 7000 Tlingit items during a single expedition. Berlin museums paid well and often rated first choice. Many of their acquired items disappeared about 1945.

Around 1890, Franz Boas, in particular, made a lasting impression on academic communities. The extensive collection attributed to him was acquired with the considerable help of George Hunt of Fort Rupert, a knowledgeable collector who was half-Tlingit.

Hunt's progeny continue to live and marry among the Kwakiutl people and carve outstanding poles to the present day.

Collectors reached into every community. In 1897, an Anglican clergyman at Masset complained in a letter to the newspaper that "every [native] grave has been rifled and the boxes that contained the bodies left strewn about." By 1910, most traditional objects of value, including many totem poles, had been removed. The Natives had been divested of almost every traditional item they owned.

As early as 1910, tourist ships travelled to Haida Gwaii and curio dealers as well as

museum curators were active in acquiring newly made native goods. Today, some museums disparagingly call these "made for tourist" items, even though at the time this was the only avenue left to traditional Natives to keep their art forms alive.

Today, there is great debate whether these collectors ultimately assisted native cultures by rescuing "evidence" before it was lost or merely accelerated their speedy decline. Much was lost or carelessly handled. In one instance, an Alaskan storekeeper, Mr. Kirberger, gathered totem poles for 25 years. His personal collection was completely destroyed by a fire in 1926. Collections that went to Berlin and St. Petersburg disappeared over the years. Several other collections were lost to museum fires in the 1900s.

The number of traditional items taken by museums expanded beyond reasonable proportions. In 1910, one researcher/collector complained in a letter to his colleague: "There is little in Alaska…I drained the Nass River [area] last year and got all that Willie [Newcombe] left… There is nothing among the Tsimshians…and you have cleaned out the Haidas." Alex Rasmussen, collector of the objects in the Portland Art Museum, declared in 1920 that British Columbia Natives had no objects of value whatsoever left from their former lives. Most of the objects, he stated, were destroyed, sold, or left behind to decay as the Native people moved into towns. Marius Barbeau, an anthropologist and avid seller of artifacts to museums, reported the same year that there were only 20 poles left intact along the Nass River. Nonetheless, he sold one in 1929 to Sir Henry Thompson. It was presented as a gift to the French government. Railway officials mistakenly "freshened up" the pole by painting it garishly before shipping.

Traditional objects and poles were scattered all over the world, some with complete, some with incomplete, documentation. It took extraordinary efforts to ship heavy totem poles, but new American and Canadian railway lines and steamship connections helped to ease the task.

It has been reported that collectors received about one dollar per inch (about 40 cents per centimetre) for a totem pole. If we use the price of gold to measure inflation (gold was about $11 an ounce then) the equivalent of a typical pole (18 to 25 metres tall) would be about $25,000—for the collector alone.

Some small amount of good did, however, emerge from the period. The impact of the non-Native influx was so great and the stoppage of traditional ways so complete, that today Native people search through museums and ethnography collections for old songs, old stories, old totem poles, old masks, and for confirmation of their traditional standards. Without these collections, much could have been forever lost.

Though mortuary figures, greet figures, and totem poles were never worshipped, early missionaries misunderstood their role and, in many cases, encouraged Natives to chop, burn, and destroy their treasures. Many that remained were snapped up by museums in the collecting frenzy of the late 1800s.

Tall

Short

Frontal

TOTEM POLES come in many shapes and sizes.

Tall freestanding poles are usually commissioned to mark a special occasion and require years of planning. The design is conceived through a collaborative process under the direction of one person, and the pole is carved by a team of apprentices under a master carver. The concepts behind tall totem poles are important, and there are layers of meaning intermingled among the figures. Status among totem poles is determined by the reputation of the chief carver, the number of consultations held with elders, and the size of the ceremony accompanying the raising. The first

freestanding poles were probably made by the Tsimshian people along the Nass and Skeena Rivers.

Short totem poles, the work of one or two carvers, illustrate a single story or one heraldic crest. This pole is the crest of a member of the Beaver clan. Its meaning can be summed up in a sentence or two. Raising ceremonies for short poles are simple affairs. Any pole, no matter how diminutive, rates a raising and blessing celebration in proportion to its size and importance.

Frontal totem poles were once carved into the load-bearing post holding the main beam of a longhouse. When height

became an issue, techniques changed. For at least 200 years, frontal poles have been constructed from separate logs, taller than the house, placed separately against the front or side of the structure. One of the original types of poles, especially popular among the Haida, these totem poles were once owned by the chief and families who occupied the home. Their presence served to announce the prestige and origins of the clans inside. This pole includes a ceremonial entrance at its base.

Greet Figures, or Welcome Poles, are based on the very first types of totem figures. Originally placed as memorials in graveyards or on beach landing sites

Greet figure

House board

Mortuary

to attract the attention of passing paddlers, today they stand at the entrance to parks, institutions, museums, or special areas.

Some greet figures have their arms outstretched; others stand arms down. A few are less human-like and feature more animal features. As their name implies, they substitute for a welcome mat, standing ever vigilant at attention and watching passers-by. This greet figure is covered with several markings.

House boards are quite rare. In their original environment, they would not have been free-standing as is the one shown here. House boards were located inside or outside the long-

house as decorative panels along the walls.

Ten to twenty of these panels decorated the inside or outside of a bighouse. House boards were particularly popular among the Coast Salish people. In previous times, this group carved a few totems, but specialized in greet figures and house boards. This particular carving was reproduced from an 1898 original and depicts a person with the power to mesmerize bears.

Mortuary poles are easily recognizable by the large panel that is said to have fronted a three-dimensional box. Said to contain the bleached remains of a high-ranking person, the box

was mounted high on the pole. It is difficult to ascertain if any of these poles actually held human remains. Even in archival photos showing newly made poles, funeral boxes seem to be missing. However, this style of construction is known as a mortuary pole and was developed among the Haida.

In native stories where these types of poles are featured, a group of friends of the deceased stands watch every night over the bones. One by one, they abandon their duties until only one person is left to defend against grave-robbers. This person then encounters the spirit of the deceased.

Roused to action by tourists who viewed the deterioration of totems alongside railway tracks, the Canadian government underwrote a restoration project in the late 1920's

Isolated Preservation Efforts: 1870 to 1940

As early as 1873, Dr. Israel Wood Powell, first Indian commissioner for British Columbia, toured coastal Native villages aboard the gunboat *Boxer*. Sensing the academic feeding frenzy about to accelerate, he strongly recommended the province of British Columbia begin an immediate collection of native art and artifacts. The plea fell on the deaf ears of a cash-strapped government. Powell was also the first to have misgivings about native Canadian items being removed to American institutions. This too met no response.

In 1889 the *Art*, Historical and Scientific Association was founded in Vancouver. Its mandate was to collect dilapidated poles, move them to Vancouver, and restore them. Evolving into the *Vancouver Museum Society* of today, this group was responsible for acquiring most of the present-day poles on display in Stanley Park.

The upper Skeena River was the site of another preservation effort. Roused to action by tourists' complaints about the serious deterioration of the remaining poles visible along the railway tracks, the federal Department of Indian Affairs, National Parks, National Museums, and the Canadian National Railway undertook the first project of its kind to restore the poles along the river. Between 1925 and 1929, about 90 percent of the poles—60 were salvageable—were restored at Hazelton, Hagwelget, Kitwancool, and Kispiox. They were re-erected (at that time), facing the railway tracks, as tourist points of interest.

A few other western Canadian conservation efforts took place between 1935 and 1940.

CNR steamships were authorized to bring intact totem poles free of charge to Prince Rupert, BC. That community began an official city-wide totem pole collection, still enjoyed today. During that period, several poles were added to Vancouver's Stanley Park

The Northwest School of Native Art is a Native-run school for Native artists and carvers founded in 1969. Many of its graduates have gone on to outstanding careers. One way to recognize the graduates of this school is their characteristic stylized depiction of a hand.

collection. A few old totem poles were erected in Victoria on a vacant lot on the corner of Bellevue and Douglas Streets, a site that later became Thunderbird Park.

Sensitized to the deterioration of native sites in Alaska, a few voices were faintly heard. As early as 1918, US Judge James Wickersham started a

fledgling movement to preserve the remaining totem poles at Port Tongass. At the same time, James G. Steese, president of the Alaska Road Commission, tried to stop road builders from destroying totem pole sites. Beginning in 1926, Alaskan forestry worker and concerned citizen Charles Florey wrote to government officials lamenting the deterioration of native sites. However, no significant action was forthcoming until 1937, when the US Forest Service commissioned a census of poles and community houses. Between 1938 and 1940, the Forestry Branch subsequently spent $200,000 on a Civilian Conservation Corps. With the help of many local Native people, they restored a number of important Alaskan totem poles and structures. The refurbished poles stand today near Ketchikan. As part of the same program, the first true Alaskan potlatch since 1900 was held in 1940 among the Kake Natives of Wrangell. At the potlatch, of-

ficially hosted by both Chief Shaikes and the US Forest Service, several new poles were commissioned. Because one was called Barbecue Raven, suspicions were roused that the new poles had lost some of their traditional meaning.

Except for isolated instances and a few funded preservation projects that employed Native and non-Native carvers—traditional totem pole building among the Natives of British Columbia and Alaska was virtually defunct for almost 50 years.

Revival of the Old Ways: 1949 to 1965

Though there were a few exceptions, after 1890, totem pole construction and the ceremonies associated with it became increasingly dormant for almost 50 years. One famous carver, Charley James (1867–1938) of Alert Bay continued to teach his children and grandchildren the old ways. His poles were recognized in academic circles and among art aficionados. In the 1940s, his granddaughter, Kwakiutl, Ellen Neel (1916-66), one of the few recognized fe-

Thunderbird tops one of several historic totem poles on display at Vancouver's Stanley Park. The first of these poles was collected about 1889; the original of this particular one was acquired in 1927. It was replicated in 1988.

Left: Blankets stacked high are for gift giving at an early potlatch in Alert Bay. As well as blankets, quantities of food, dishes, canoes, and other trade goods were given away. This Kwakiutl community continued its practices in spite of a Canadian law banning "gift giving." Right: In 1921, sewing machine and furniture giveaways, so outraged authorities, that they came in and seized all the community's potlatch masks and traditional regalia.

male totem pole carvers, lived in Vancouver and made a meagre living producing high-quality miniature totem poles. About this time, academics at the University of British Columbia (UBC), planning Western Canada's first museum dedicated to native artifacts, realized the lamentable state of Northwest Coast native heritage-art. Obtaining a small grant in 1949, they hired Neel to restore seven salvaged totem poles. There was no standard technology or methodology for restoration work, and the task was daunting. Neel began work and solicited the help of her step-uncle Mungo Martin—another Kwakiutl student of Charley James. Within a short time it was ascertained that duplicating totem poles using new logs was more satisfactory than attempting to restore old poles through intense labour. Martin quickly eclipsed Ellen Neel, and his fame spread. He became the "Father of Totem Pole Revival" in the twentieth century.

Neel continued her efforts for native art, training her son David Neel until his untimely death in 1960. She collaborated with anthropologist Marius Barbeau and spoke at numerous university convocations and conferences. In addition to thousands of miniatures, Neel went on to carve full-sized poles for Stratford, Ontario, and the Museum of Copenhagen in Denmark. She carved five major poles for western Canada's Woodwards' stores. Though she conceived and helped to promote the idea of Vancouver marketing itself as "Totemland," her valiant first contributions are usually overlooked. In spite of the overwhelming publicity her famous relative Mungo Martin continued to receive, and in spite of the fact that she predated him and acted as his mentor, Canada Council turned down a request to fund her totem pole projects as late as 1960. She died in disappointment in 1966.

By 1947, several circles of academics, including E.W. Hamber, Chancellor of UBC, were aware that potlatch tradi-

tions and accompanying totem pole making were in serious decline or completely lost. Beginning in 1950, a UBC academic committee and provincial anthropologist Wilson Duff spearheaded a three-year project to bring totem pole traditions back from the brink of extinction. Under the direction of chief carver Mungo Martin and his son David, a team of apprentices was assembled in Victoria. Their names still read like a "Who's Who" of native art: Bill Reid, Henry Hunt, and his son Tony Hunt. About 13 replicas of totem poles were produced and raised with appropriate ceremonies. Elders from outlying communities travelled to Victoria to perform traditional raising ceremonies. When funding ran out, the Victoria Times Colonist newspaper organized a community donation project. In 1953, a large ceremonial bighouse, officially named Old 'Naḵa'pan̲kam̲', was built in the centre of Victoria and dedicated to Martin's family-clans in perpetuity. The elaborate and authentic potlatch dedication ceremony attracted elders from throughout British Columbia. The public almost stampeded the ceremonies, and anthropologists declared that a wealth of native dances and traditions, previously unknown, had been revived. The bighouse structure was constructed to shelter Martin's restoration work and to show gratitude for his contribution to the people of British Columbia and the world.

With replication projects well underway, it was not long before the subject of tall totem poles returned to the forefront. In 1956, Martin and his team raised the world's tallest totem pole—38.9 metres (127 feet, 7 inches). Located in Beacon Hill Park, Victoria, it was

designed to pay tribute to Canada's World War II Native war veterans. With word of the world's tallest spreading through the media, orders for totem poles poured in from museums, governments, and private citizens. Mungo Martin and his team carved two identical centennial poles. In 1958, one was presented to Queen Elizabeth II and the British royal family in London, England. They are exactly 100 feet (30 metres) tall. The Colony of New Caledonia, later called British Columbia was established in 1858. The duplicate centennial pole was raised in front of the Maritime Museum in Vancouver.

In 1959, David Martin, Mungo's son and chosen successor, accidentally drowned. Martin remained stoic. After giving the situation considerable thought, he decided to turn over what would have been his son's legacy to the provincial museum. In addition to masks, personal regalia, and totem poles, he also donated his copper, symbol of his authority and wealth.

Having revived excellence in native arts and having taught several other apprentices, Martin passed away in

In the late 1930s, the US Forest Service dispelled disparaging rumours of the day that a slave's bones were buried at the base of old totem poles. Many original poles were dug up, but no trace of bones was ever discovered. Today, a silver dollar is buried at the base of some poles.

1962. His body lay in state and was returned with great ceremony to his chosen place in Alert Bay. Soon after, his community began plans to construct the world's highest totem pole in his honour. To continue Martin's work in Victoria, Henry Holt was appointed chief provincial carver. The Alert Bay band fulfilled its plan in 1980, when a 53.7 metre (173 foot) world-record pole was raised.

The Canada Council posthumously awarded its highest medal to Martin in 1963, but plans for various memorial plaques in Vancouver and Victoria never came to pass. The provincial government eventually commissioned a small 9.8 metre (32 foot) memorial pole in his honour in 1970. It was raised in the Alert Bay cemetery where he is buried.

Public Appreciation Grows: 1955 to 1975

Meanwhile, Martin's apprentices began several projects of their own. Bill Reid, a soon-to-be famous Haida artist, first travelled to Haida Gwaii in 1957 to assess the poles there. He then returned to oversee a three-and-a-half year university-sponsored project with Kwakiutl artist Douglas Cranmer. Together, they oversaw the construction of the native-style houses and carved totem poles now in place outside the Museum of Anthropology in Vancouver.

During the 1960s and 1970s, commercial businesses, government bodies, and other institutions began to appreciate the uniqueness of this ancient art form. Scores of poles were commissioned. The Boy Scouts of Canada commissioned a pole for their new headquarters in Ottawa. Woodwards' stores employed Ellen Neel to construct five poles for their stores. The province of British Columbia commissioned 11 Native carvers and their assistants to build 19 poles to be placed along BC highways and at ferry terminals. The Canadian government commissioned poles for some of its embassies and

Miniature Totem Poles

MINIATURE TOTEM POLES are sold in souvenir stores. However, they play a greater part in the totem pole tradition than many tourists suspect. Before a full-sized pole is constructed, miniature versions are carved to check out the effect and to gain the approval of the chiefs and elders who have commissioned the pole. If the carver has inadvertently carved an offending story figure or crest, the figure can be modified before a full-sized rendition is made. These mini-poles have value on their own.

In past times, when a totem pole was destroyed, it was sometimes replicated secretly in miniature form, to remember it before time obscured its features. Many traditional Haida totem poles claimed by destruction or decay are known only by miniature argillite poles carved in remembrance of them.

This archival photo shows pole carver Opitsit, a carver about 1920, working on miniatures that will be approved and later carved into full-sized totem poles.

as national gifts. Juneau, Alaska, marked its 1972 centenary with two authentic poles.

During this era, new precedents concerning the collecting of native art were established, and these are still followed today. No longer can totem poles be expropriated. In 1958, for example, Gitksan village chiefs allowed some of their poles to be removed to a museum for preservation. Their conditions stated that the poles be replicated and returned. They were. A totem pole, on display at Expo '70 in Osaka, Japan, was returned after the fair was over. At the time of this writing, the Museum of Civilization in Ottawa is unable to persuade Kitwancool village elders to relinquish the famous Hole-in-Ice pole, one of the oldest in the world.

A renaissance in excellence emerged. To encourage young carvers, the Kwakiutl Arts and Crafts Foundation began in Alert Bay. Young artist and carver Robert Davidson returned to his roots and in 1969 raised the first new pole in Haida Gwaii in 50 years. This was followed in 1984 by a Bill Reid pole. An accredited school of Northwest Coast native art was founded in 1969 near Hazelton. Museums throughout the world re-evaluated their totem pole collections and realized the extent of their treasures. The Museum of Anthropology at UBC opened in 1962 with a comprehensive collection of indoor totem poles. Later the museum hosted a year-long exhibition of Norman Tait totem poles. In Kake, Alaska, a tall pole, 45.7 metres high (150 feet high), was raised, and a number of older poles from around Alaska were assembled at the new Ketchikan Heritage Centre. 'Ksan, a re-created native village in northern British Columbia, opened with great fanfare.

New names emerged as proficiency increased: Norman Tait (Nisga'a Tsimshian), Richard Hunt (Kwakiutl) and Calvin Hunt (Kwakiutl), Bob Neel—son of Ellen Neel (Kwakiutl), Joe David (Nootka), Art Thompson (Nootka), Robert Davidson (Haida), and Nathan Jackson (Tlingit).

Public appreciation for totem pole carving gradually increased, but sadly, several impostors began to take advantage of the public's overall lack of familiarity with the tradition. True totem poles are the work of Northwest Coast Natives. Totem crests and the retelling of narratives are the prerogative of Native carvers and their apprentices. Completed poles must be raised and blessed with appropriate ceremonies conducted by Northwest Coast band elders. However several "fake" totem poles made both by Natives and non-Natives from completely unrelated traditions continued to appear in public

Tall totem poles are important for boasting rights, but they do not photograph very well. This 38.9 metre (127 foot, 7 inch) pole erected in 1956 at Beacon Hill in Victoria, once held the record as the world's tallest totem pole. As of 1995, it is surpassed in height by two taller poles—one in Kake, Alaska 45.7 metres (150 feet), and the tallest in the world at Alert Bay at 52.7 metres (173 feet).

places—usually outside British Columbia and Alaska.

Unfortunately, opportunistic artists using chain saws continue to turn out "totems." Several people who never knew Mungo Martin masquerade as one of his trainees. One unsanctioned pole carved by an Ontario non-Native man (married to an eastern Canadian Native woman) stands prominently in the centre of Banff, Alberta.

Native Art by and for Native People: 1980 to Present

In the 1980s and 1990s Natives gradually began to operate their own tourism establishments. Realizing the public appeal of their own art and heritage, Natives opened their Kwagiulth Museum and Cultural Centre on Quadra Island. The abandoned Ninstints (Skungwaii) village was declared a World Heritage Site and is administered by the Haida. Kiks'adi Totem Park and Saxman Village in Alaska were dedicated. To celebrate

the momentous occasion of raising the world's tallest totem in 1980, Alert Bay's collection of potlatch treasures, confiscated by the government in 1922, were returned to the Kwakiutl people. A great ceremony followed. The treasures remain on permanent display at the U'mista Cultural Centre. In 1983, Duncan, BC, declared itself the City of Totems and set up a perpetual totem pole carving regime among the Cowichan people. They in turn opened the Native Heritage Centre, complete with a carving shed to shelter totem pole carvers year-round. Thirty-

How Old are Totem Poles?

Elder Robert Good views a replication of Hole-In-Ice, a pole once reputed to be one of the oldest "still standing".

TOTEM POLES ARE generally constructed from untreated cedar logs. Though cedar is resistant to insects and fungi, the effect of weathering is relentless. After 70 to 100 years battling the elements, totem poles tend to decay and fall over. An old totem is the responsibility of the descendants of the family that erected it. Until

that family can afford to commission a duplicate, the spent totem may lie on the ground. It has not been forgotten. When arrangements are completed, family carvers are appointed. The old pole is carefully moved to a carving shed, such as the one pictured, and a duplicate is made. If there are no talented carvers in

the owner's clan, outsiders may be appointed. However, in that case, an appointed family member must "stand over" the hired carvers during every moment of the process. In the end, the re-carved pole becomes a symbol of honour for the family.

nine properly dedicated totem poles stood in Duncan by 1994.

Museums have slowly instituted new policies. For example, the Museum of Anthropology in Vancouver loans out its artifacts to Natives for use during their potlatches, and many important items have been returned to the people. Museums throughout North America, including the American Museum of Natural History, are reviewing requests by native people to return all or part of their collections. In 1993, the Anglican Church of Canada made a much publicized return of its confiscated Kwakiutl treasures.

Northwest Coast native art continues its slow renaissance in the world outside the region. In Paris, in 1992, a major exhibition was mounted. A team of traditional canoeists travelled up the Seine River, and the art received widespread acclaim. Bill Reid's art and jewellry has increased 10-fold in value in less than a decade. The names of other native artists have become recognized in non-Native settings. In 1993, a statue designed by Bill Reid was placed in front of the Canadian embassy in Washington, DC, drawing outstanding and appreciative public reviews.

The quality and fluid lines of authentic Northwest Coast native art as it has evolved from the mists of ancient times to the present day continue to bring pleasure to onlookers. The art of totem pole building continues to be an important part of that tradition.

Two Haida houses on the grounds of the Museum of Anthropology at UBC represent a family dwelling and a small mortuary chamber. The poles were constructed by Bill Reid (Haida) and Douglas Cranmer (Kwakiutl). In former times, a typical Native village consisted of about 50 such buildings, each housing a dozen or so families.

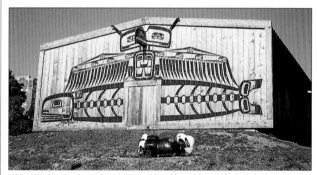

Alert Bay, the final resting place of Mungo Martin, is a predominantly Native community. It is home to the U'mista Cultural Centre housing treasures of the potlatch, a totem pole that was one the world's tallest totem pole, and a longhouse.

Built in the style of a Kwakiutl bighouse, this building in the centre of Victoria was dedicated by potlatch in perpetuity to Mungo Martin and his family clan. It is only opened during ceremonial periods, but can be viewed from the outside at anytime.

2. Totem Pole Symbols and Ceremonies

A glint of sun hints at Thunderbird's traditional power to control lightning

Totem pole symbolism is intimately linked to the kinship system of the Northwest Coast. The family relationship, as defined among members of a group, is called its kinship system. The familiar Western kinship system of mother-father, brother-sister, uncle-aunt, niece-nephew, sister-in-law and brother-in-law, is based on European convention and law, as well as on blood relationship. The common system of surname transfer, for example, is generally based on the recognition of the father's or one parent's paternal line of ancestry. In the recent past, a woman used to automatically drop her own surname at marriage and take her husband's. Lately, some children inherit double surnames—including the wife's birth surname. This is based on an evolving, but yet imperfect, method to interweave the maternal line into a paternal system. However, if after two generations of hyphenated surnames, the last name becomes unwieldy,will the female line name be dropped?

Northwest Coast tribal groups before contact had evolved a kinship system that featured some of the same rules as the European system and some of their own conventions. As individuals did not have surnames as we know them, and with four or more marriages common among women, the transfer of prerogatives based on parentage was complex. For example, the system of passing names was generally through the maternal line, and inheritance or wealth was often passed from a man to his nephew, not his son. Names were often assigned rather than transferred. Certain names were split in half

Natural

Painted

Feathering

FEATHERING IS A special technique much favoured by several Native artists. Done with a small adze, the "chipping" technique covers the entire surface and takes a great deal of time. However, the finish lends a richness to the surface, particularly evident as the pole ages. Feathering is an "optional extra" on particularly valuable poles, adding a patina of quality to the pole.

Grain blasting is a new technique just beginning to come into favour among artists. When a particularly attractive grain is revealed, gentle sand blasting is used to bring the grain into high focus. Here, the blasting was skillfully done, after the feathering details were first masked off.

A natural smooth finish remains a favoured technique. Without any paint at all, the natural carved shapes and wood grain of the pole come into high focus. When a pole is new, its natural colour is yellow-blond or reddish-blond. Cedar wood ages in about two years to a characteristic silver-grey. It is normal for

Grain Blasting

poles to crack with age, and various techniques are now used to periodically fill the cracks and sand them smooth. Some people prefer poles with natural cracks.

Painted surfaces were once popular but are becoming less fashionable. Inspired by the bleached remains of old poles, modern artists increasingly use coloured paint only as accents or not at all. The Kwakiutl people

continue to produce poles with the greatest number of painted and add-on pieces. Painted poles also suffer the effects of weathering and need frequent repainting if they are to appear new and bright. Some say they like the weathered look, and others enjoy a totem best when it is freshly painted.

and one syllable transferred from one name and one syllable from another. Though lineage was generally based on the maternal line, occasionally a complex combination of the two lines could be arranged. For example, in some groups the inherited privileges of a wife's ancestors could be passed as a gift to a husband by his wife's father. However, the mother's genealogy was always paramount.

Phratries are the political-kinship divisions of people tied both by blood and by the need to band together as a tribe for protection. Banding together to form a community, these people then begin to claim descent from a common ancestor. In other cultures, specifi-cally among the Scottish or the Irish, such groups are known as clans. For describing the Kwakiutl people only, Franz Boas, an early anthropologist, coined the term *numaym*. In this book, the more widely used terms of "phratry" and "clan" are used interchangeably for all Northwest Coast kinship divisions.

Phratries or Kinship Groups

"Phratry" is an academic term used for tribal people along the Pacific northwest coast. Kinship groups associate together and claim descent from a common ancestor, who may be non-human. Phratry association can be passed by blood or by assignment during a public ceremony. For example, a person not previously a member of an Eagle phratry could be declared a member and thus claim descent from Eagle. This is somewhat similar to our present-day adoption system.

Phratry associations were not only based on blood relationships but also on the need for certain families to see themselves as intimately related for the purposes of defending themselves against common enemies and of working together to collect food and provide a comfortable lifestyle. The addition of political or protective connections to the family line is not widely recognized in Western society. However, it was essential among Native groups. Each of these groups of people

Linkages: Nature and Totem Art

THE FIRST FORCES that inspired carvers to create the characteristic shapes seen in Northwest Coast native art are lost in the mists of time. But a walk along the beaches and in the rainforests of Alaska and British Columbia conjures up shapes and figures that may show a link between the land and the art of the people. Powered by a small degree of imagination, it is possible to see beached logs taking on animal forms, knots in trees with faces, shadows playing into shapes very much like those seen in the works of master carvers. The appeal of Northwest Coast art may be that it strikes a deep cord of recognition and seems to show humanity's oneness with nature. The figures shown here are a Gitksan totem rendition of Mosquito and a strongly reminiscent piece of driftwood.

Story

Commemorative

Pride

TOTEM POLES ARE MORE than stories. Hidden among the figures are layers of intertwined meaning. One figure may represent more than one thing. For example, Bear may be a family crest, the telling of Bear's story, or a lesson to remind Native people that self-sacrifice is desirable. Furthermore, the whole pole may be a memorial to an honoured elder or serve as testimony that the carver has, for example, overcome an addictive habit.

Narrative Story Rights or Story Figures

Certain figures appear on totem poles as a symbol of the owner's rights to tell the stories or sing the songs associated with one's phratry or family kinship. These figures include the popular Bear, who represents a common story with wide rights of telling, or Raven and one of his cycle of stories. Southern bands carve poles with more narrative figures. Today, stories are told freely without much regard to traditional rights. The story pole shown here illustrates the famous story of Bear-Mother. (See Chapter 3 for a complete telling of this story.)

Remembrance of Heroic Events

In some cases, the figures on totem poles are meant to recall a heroic exploit, the sufferings of a brave person, or a memorable disaster such as a flood or volcanic eruption. Since the events are primarily important to Native people, they are not always familiar to outsiders. However, the photo here shows a commemorative pole erected to a modern non-Native hero, Rick Hansen, a wheelchair athlete who wheeled around the world over a two-year period raising millions of dollars for spinal cord research.

Pride in One's Native Heritage

The outstanding art form that totem pole carving embodies has advanced to the point where modern artists carve poles with loose relationships to past practices. Tribal styles are liberally interpreted; stories are given new twists; phratry crests are included with or without rights. While purists may express concern about these practices, there are so many talented artists and so many wonderful stories full of life and movement that the natural progression of the art form is toward the expression of the tradition as pride in one's heritage. On these poles, the artist simply declares what the pole represents. There is less need to resort to strict protocol. The photo here shows a totem pole expressing various native concepts of transformation, some heraldic figures, and the need for cooperation between people.

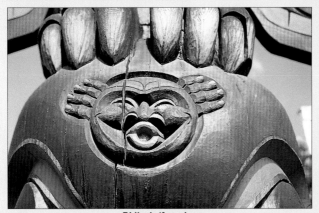
Ridicule/Amusing

Heraldic

Ridicule, Shaming, or Amusing Acts

In a few cases, totem poles contain figures meant to shame the owner of the pole. If the carvers were not paid, if the family owed debts, or if protocol was breached in a serious manner, the rules of totem pole carving were deliberately broken. In most cases, outsiders cannot see the breach, but Native people can. To greatly insult the owner, a figure might be visibly carved upside down or embarrassingly naked. Ridicule poles are rare because the owners generally do not raise them. In a few cases, mistakes or figures are added simply to create amusement. The photo here shows a humorous figure, in this case, meant to amuse rather than ridicule.

Mortuary or Memorial Remembrances

Among coastal First Nations, totem poles continue to be raised at a great potlatch in the years following the death of an influential elder. The totem serves both as a remembrance for the family and an announcement of their rights. Traditionally, northern bands carved more totem poles serving strictly as memorials than their neighbours to the south. A few included mortuary boxes constructed to hold the last remains of the deceased. Shown here is a mortuary pole, which in the old days would have fronted a mortuary box.

Kinship Rights or Heraldic Crests

Certain figures appear on a totem pole announcing the right of the owner to display a symbol associated with their moiety relationship or phratry. Outsiders sometimes compare these to clan surnames. These kinship symbols were passed by blood through the maternal line or were granted to a person during public ceremonies. Heraldic crest figures include various mythological beings such as Siskiutl, Copper Woman, and Moon Crest, as well as various animals such as Double-Finned Whale or Giant Beaver. Northern bands carve poles with more heraldic crest symbols and fewer narrative figures. The heraldic pole shown here consists almost entirely of the Frog heraldic crest repeated over and over.

Mortuary

45

Here dancers pose in the costumes they use for dancing ceremonies and rituals stretching late into the night. Young initiates receive affirmation of the traditions of their ancestors.

claimed similar attributes, symbolized by displaying certain animals or mythological figures.

Moieties

Moieties are the largest phratry divisions in a tribe, or approximately the largest "half and half" divisions among bands. For example, all the members of one tribe might belong to either the Wolf or the Raven moiety. Additionally, there may be 50 to 100 subdivisions under the two major divisions. Each of these subdivisions has the right to display certain totemic figures, but not others. Each person is allowed to display their major moiety symbol and a variable number of the submoiety symbols based on kinship and property rights. To the present day, when outsiders ask a Native person about his or her Native name

or clan associations, it is a difficult question. Most Natives give simplistic answers to what is a very complex situation. Others leave their clan associations and rights for their elders to sort out. "Ask my auntie," they say.

Titles

Titles are a series of ranked positions that were generally inherited through the maternal line. Interest in property came through the male lines; kinship rights through female lines. Titles could be earned by an individual who had an encounter with a supreme being or in recognition of a contribution to the group. Among the Kwakiutl people, for example, during the nineteenth century, there were about 900 titled positions. Titling rules were complex. Native people operated under an oral (not a written)

tradition. Thus there was no official "rights and privileges registry office." Rather, the granting of a title was symbolized by the right to display certain totemic figures and the process verified by an official witness. These powers, privileges, and interests in property were then symbolized by the right to

a) be called a certain name and claim descent from a certain phratry
b) perform certain dances and sing certain songs
c) tell certain stories

This bestowing according to the laws of kinship was then symbolized by displaying sanctioned totemic figures on one's dishes, clothing, weapons, and totem poles. Great offense was taken if anyone displayed a figure to which they had no rights.

Exogamic Marriages

Exogamic marriages are the custom of marrying outside one's own close kinship group. This is widely practised around the world, but the definition of who is "close" varies. There were strict exogamic rules among the various phratries along the Northwest Coast. However, these rules arose from a combination of heraldic crests and property rights. Therefore, one was sometimes entitled to marry a person who might be considered taboo in Western society, and by the same rights others were off-limits under the totemic system who were considered unrelated in the Western system.

The System of Witnessing

All this complex granting of names, rights, privileges, and the symbolism associated with it had to be recorded. In a society without a written language, this could be a complex task. Therefore, a whole system of witnesses and witnessing arose to keep track of the kinship, marriage eligibility, and property transference. At each public ceremony, a witness or a group of witnesses was formally appointed for each portion of the ceremony. These groups of persons were entrusted with the duty to watch carefully, memorize a portion of the proceedings, and give a first-hand accounting of the granting of a kinship right or property rights whenever asked to do so. The witness-person or witness-group could be called on at a later date to verify that a privilege had indeed been publicly granted. To be certain that the witnesses paid strict attention during the

This armorial bearing has meaning within the British heraldry system. The arms are registered with a central body that approves the design and sanctions the right to officially display it. No two registered coat of arms are identical, and each symbol has meaning. In many ways, this practice corresponds to the traditional native system for sanctioning totem figures.

Common Practices

The practice of associating under animal symbols is not exclusive to Native people. Even in Western society, groups of people band together for common purposes under animal symbols. For example, the Fraternal Order of Eagles, the Lions Clubs International, and the Elks Lodges consist of like-minded people who help each other and society, especially those most in need of protection—its underprivileged. Cities, municipalities, and individual families often commission an armorial bearing or a coat of arms that symbolizes the characteristics identified with the city or family; these are strictly defined under the British or German heraldic systems.

long ceremonies, they were given lavish gifts. This was to attract their attention, to thank them, to perpetuate a sense of belonging, and to compensate them (in advance) should they ever need to travel back to bear witness in a dispute over property or kinship.

Rights, Symbols, and Heraldic Crests

Ethnographers commonly accept totemism as a type of social organization that defines lines of kinship and records them for posterity. Under totemic rules, there are definitions about whom one may or may not consider as a marriage partner, based on who has and who has not the right to claim association with certain totem figures. In ancient times, there were also little-mentioned (and imperfectly followed) practices within totemism, such as certain taboos against eating one's totem animals.

Within the totemic or phratry system, a totem animal or supernatural figure is variously regarded as the blood-line parent of the group or, in certain circumstances, as having granted rights to the group by association. Exogamic marriages were sanctioned, and

Prominent symbols displayed on native ceremonial clothing and on totem poles serve to announce a person's rank, prestige, and kinship relationships.

Hints for "Reading" Totem Poles

1. Create an imaginary line from west to east across the northern tip of Vancouver Island. Totem poles *north* of this line consist mainly of heraldic crests with a few story figures carved in for contrast. Totem poles *south* of this line are mainly story figures with a heraldic crest or two interwoven among the figures.

2. Older totem poles show more heraldic crests and fewer story figures.

3. Modern totem poles show more story figures and fewer heraldic crests.

4. Modern poles commissioned for non-Natives are concerned with art, line, and form, and tend to consist of story figures. The artists and carvers may or may not include their personal heraldic crests.

5. Totem poles commissioned for Native use are careful to follow heraldic crest rules as well as strict story lines.

members of each clan were considered to have certain rights, privileges, and prohibitions stemming from their phratry associations. The etiquette and protocol based on rights was complex. When a large gathering of many clans met, there were hundreds of conventions to be observed. It was easy to inadvertently insult someone. As a result of the regulations and privileges within the totemic system, planning for a potlatch was as complex as the modern equivalent of planning protocol for a visit from British and Arabic royalty—at once.

Each right, privilege, and kinship association was publicly noted by displaying certain heraldic crests or narrative figures on one's privately owned articles and, in later times, the carving of those symbols onto totem poles. Because a person spent a whole lifetime accumulating rights and heraldic crests, sometimes the sum of one's symbolic figures might not be carved onto a totem pole until after one's death. Then the pole with its heraldic crests and figures served as an announcement of the departed's total family-line rights to be passed on to future generations.

Still later, other minor symbols were intertwined into totem poles. These include statements of ridicule and commemorative stories of great events. In modern times, the passing of phratry rights among Natives is being revived. However, totem pole figures carved for non-Natives and public institutions do not represent phratry rights but are the evolution of an outstanding art form.

The crest of the exclusive Vancouver Club symbolizes its links with Canadian history (the beaver trade), its association with British royalty (the crown), and its perceived prestige (the subdued effect of the total crest). In some ways, this corresponds to the traditional native system and the prestige associated with displaying certain totemic figures.

The Potlatch

The potlatch celebration is the oldest and most important festival among the Natives of the Northwest Coast. In previous times, it sustained their ranking system and brought a sense of order to the system. In the present day, it perpetuates a sense of belonging.

A gathering to which people were invited to share food for a betrothal or a birth was called a "feast". A potlatch is a gathering where people were called upon to bear witness to a myriad of legal matters and to receive gifts. In early times, potlatches might be held once a decade. After European contact, with the greater dissemination of trade goods and the emergence of a nouveau riche class, potlatches might be held every two years or so. There was no fixed schedule for potlatching. Elders called a potlatch when they were ready. Much misunderstood by outsiders, the potlatch was a time of affirming social rank, taking care of important legal matters, establishing a sense of order in the society, and providing for the redistribution of goods from the few to the many in order to impress one's rise in station on others.

forms and the pole is slowly moved to the exact place where it will stand. In this way, as it moves, the totem pole becomes part of the people.

16. In some ceremonies, more invocations are said and more songs are sung. Here, helpers strain while final preparations are made for the final hoisting. Because this pole is small, it was simply dropped into a metal ring holder. In early times, a sloping pit was dug and poles were gradually eased into the upright position using overhead ropes and backfill.

17. Today, modern technology is a bonus for moving larger poles into position. Cranes and skyhooks make the job an easier one, though the starting and stopping of the machine can create anxious moments for the spectators.

18. Even with the help of modern technology, the carvers and their teams of helpers always seem to experience some worrying moments. There are ongoing concerns, both for the safety of the surrounding public, who invariably press too close, and for the carver, who, like the anxious bride at a wedding, is asked in detail what he or she wants at every step of the pole placement.

19. Small poles rate small ceremonies; important poles rate important ceremonies. The status of a totem pole is bound up with the reputation of the carver, the prestige of the owner, and the number of elders and appropriate dignitaries the raising ceremony attracts. Small commercial poles such as this one being raised in front of a gift shop rate appropriately sized ceremonies.

20. After the upright totem pole is in place, dance ceremonies take place. The carvers and their families are given places of honour, as are the owners of the pole. The Native people then give out gifts, usually fresh apples and oranges, to the crowd as a gesture of thanks for bearing witness to the raising of the pole. The feasting that follows goes on late into the night.

3. Identifying Totem Figures

Bear glows as the sun sets

I n 1909, John Reed Swanton, an anthropologist, identified and catalogued 62 Haida heraldic crests. A few years later, in 1916, Franz Boas, a collector and an ethnographer, reported on 99 different Tsimshian heraldic crests. Each of these crests is carved onto at least one totem pole. Since that time,

many potlatches have been held and the number of heraldic crests sanctioned among all Northwest Coast Native nations has increased. Therefore, the figures listed alphabetically in this chapter do not cover every heraldic image and story figure carved onto every totem pole in British Columbia and Alaska. Instead, the listings are representative of some of the common figures a viewer is likely to encounter. Any given totem pole is likely to display several additional figures whose exact meaning is

known only to the carvers and the owners of the pole.

For a century between 1840 and 1940, early anthropologists and ethnographers travelled among the people collecting objects and recording their family stories and songs. The stories condensed in this section are derived from early recorded accounts. In each case, an academic researcher interviewed Native subjects who recounted stories as they were handed down from their grandparents and great-grandparents. Some of these stories,

therefore, may stretch back to precontact times. Many are the retellings of stories originating long before that. In the decades since these stories were first collected, they have been subject to "re-editing" to reflect current thinking. Particularly in recent years, traditional stories are being completely reinterpreted. With the exception of Thunderbird's story, which is modern, the stories in this chapter are the retelling of compilations based on early recorded accounts freely given to museum and

IN THE TIME before this, it was berry season and the women ventured far from the village to harvest the crop. Among their numbers was a princess, daughter of a great chief, who was unaccustomed to such work. The spoiled girl begged her father to let her go adventuring with the women, and he reluctantly agreed. All day she had problems. First, she stepped in bear excrement. Breaking a taboo specifying that no Bear should be insulted, she complained long and bitterly. Her companions fell silent. When it was evening and time to return home, her headstrap broke three times, her basket spilled, and she fell behind. Frantically seeking her agile companions, she encountered a handsome young man who offered to carry her basket and take her to his village before dark. She was pleased to go with him.

After a long walk, the two arrived at an odd village inhabited by people wearing bearskin garments. The princess was introduced to her companion's father, the Bear-Chief, who treated her kindly. While the slaves were preparing her dinner, Mouse-woman crept to her side with pertinent information on her predicament—the princess was a prisoner of the Bears, who would shortly assume their normal appearance. Mouse-woman advised her to cooperate and gave her

procedural hints to avoid becoming their slave. (These rituals form a significant part of the story, but they are not related here.) The princess followed Mouse-woman's directions to the letter.

Back in her own village, her people were grief-stricken. Her four brothers and a dog set out to find her. Each killed many bears during his search, and the first three brothers were unsuccessful in their quests.(The brothers' adventures form a significant part of the story, but they are not related here.)

Unlike the heroine in *Beauty and the Beast,* the young woman easily adapted to living with

Bears manifesting in their own shape and size. Bear-Prince asked for her hand. They were duly married, with a proper ceremony, and soon she gave birth to Bear twins. She was a devoted mother, and the boys grew quickly. When it became known how many Bear brethren were being killed in her name, her caring Bear husband decided to move the family to a more secure location. They travelled high into the mountains where they lived quite happily. The Bear-Prince performed certain rituals to insure their safety. (These form a significant part of the story, but they are not related here.)

When the rescue team under the direction of her fourth (and weakest) brother was finally sighted, the princess pressed her fingerprints into a snowball and rolled it down the mountain to attract their attention. Her rescue was at hand. Just before her husband, the Bear-Prince was killed, he asked to sing a dirge by which he might be remembered. His wish was granted and as he died he pulled the bearskins from his children, making them manifest in their human form.

Bear-Mother and her offspring returned to her human village, founding the first generations of the Bear clan. There are supplementary stories about her unhappiness and the family's periodic return to the Bear's village.

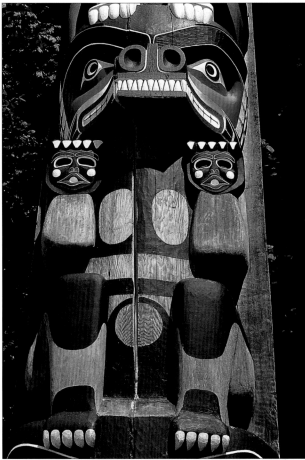

Bear represents a spirit of noble self-sacrifice

ing Bear characters are performed in many First Nations groups and both Bear-as-a-foster-parent and Bear-as-a-spouse stories are common. Bear medicine is known to have curative powers, and some shamans can transform themselves into Bear. Some of the oldest artifacts recovered on the West Coast include a shaman's crown made of bear claws.

Bear is not a mere animal to be admired or hunted, but also a semidivinity. Its ability to form a link between humans and the spirit world is a common thread between many cultures. Bear stories are very ancient.

Bear's Appearance

Totem Bear is distinguished by its ears (if present), snout, teeth, eyebrows, and paws. The ears are flattened in an inverted U-shape, often containing smaller decorations or little bears inside. In earlier times, its teeth were not always defined, but modern carvers show Bear teeth with prominent incisors. Eyes are well defined and feature eyebrows. Many Bears sit upright, and Bear-Mother holds a human-looking child in her arms. If Bear's animal nature is uppermost, its paws are shown, its claws are well defined, and smaller figures appear on its pads. If the shape-shifting abilities of Bear are illustrated, it has a combination of human features and animal-human appendages.

university researchers.

Cautionary Note: These stories are not suitable for children. They are the oral stories that give meaning to the kinship systems of Northwest Coast Native people. They contain many stated or implied concepts suitable for mature minds.

Bear and Bear-Mother

Bear and Bear-Mother are prevalent players in many mythologies. In the western world, bear stories such as *Why Bear has No Tail* and *The Three Bears* are passed on through fairy tales. However, Bear is a more serious creature in aboriginal cultures. Bear ceremonies, as well as Bear images, are particularly well developed in Siberia and among the Inuit people of the North. The Ainu of Japan pay extensive homage to Bear. Mimetic dances and ceremonies featur-

> *"…That I may…take hold of your left paw…to inherit your power of getting easily with your hands the salmon that you catch."*
> — *Kwakiutl, Chant to a Black Bear*

Bear's Personality and Habits

Bears live in families, and have brothers, sisters, chiefs, slaves, wives, and husbands just as people do. They live in social communities, understand religious taboos, love their children, hold marriage ceremonies, and mourn the death of their brethren. They hold meetings and seek each other's advice. Like humans, they go out hunting in the day, have meals, celebrate life events, accept and give gifts, and value copper as a commodity. They venture out on occasional slave raids but they capture humans—not other Bears. Unlike humans, Bears build their hearth fires with very wet wood because they have the ability to keep it alight; dry wood goes out when they ignite it. They hibernate in winter. Most Bear households shelter a wise talking rodent, Mouse-woman, as a sort of permanent houseguest. She knows all their deepest secrets.

Bear Powers

Like all other animals, Bears have the power to take their skins off and appear as human beings do. Most of the time, however, they prefer their own form. They are quite perceptive in knowing when human hunters are after them, and a few have a precognition of their own death. Of great importance is their ability to mate with humans, who then give birth to twin offspring. The children grow from babyhood to young adolescence in record time, can assume either parent's form at will, enjoy the company of either their mother's or their father's families, and exhibit the best abilities of both Bears and humans. However, Bear children marry humans. It is these offspring who founded the first "human" Bear clan families.

Today, these phratries have expanded to include new heraldic crests such as Bear-of-the-Sea, and many phratries have inherited the right to carve Bear as a story figure. In the strictest totemic tradition, kinsfolk never ate or hunted their totem animal. In practice, this was sometimes circumvented by claiming the animal killed was only a "natural" bear, not a Bear.

"Welcome, friend, Throwing-down-in-One-Day, you Tree-Feller, for you have agreed to come to me…that you may give me your ability to work…for nothing is impossible for you to work at."
—Kwakiutl, Chant to Beaver after It Has Been Killed

Bear's Relationship with Humans

Though humans are their enemies, Bears appreciate human awe. They are aware of the taboos and ceremonies humans hold in their honour, and they are annoyed when humans utter insults against their dignity. Both groups tend to

This pole represents Beaver's return as a revered animal in place of its former status as rival.

A little Bear peaks out from an adult Bear's ears

avoid each other except during berry season when they uneasily frequent the same berry patches. Rank-and-file Bears marry their own kind, but occasionally a Bear-Chief's son falls in love with a human female—always a high-ranking chief's daughter. He is a faithful husband and a dutiful father in spite of being fully aware of his in-laws' murderous intents. His offspring eventually go to live with the human side of their family. Their progeny are humans but are intimately related to Bears and therefore owe Bears special homage and favours in return for their special powers.

Beaver

Beaver is a story character and heraldic crest among Native people who engaged in the fur trade. With the arrival of Europeans, the search for fur-bearing animals was so enhanced that hunting areas became the subject of great rivalries. The desire for wealth created a productive industry. The system of heraldic crests signifying the right to trade in pelts was a serious matter. To this day, the Beaver is Canada's national emblem.

Native Beaver clans on the West Coast can trace their origins to about 1830, when the Hudson's Bay Company became active in fur trading west of the Rockies. Adapting HBC's royal emblem, several members of the Eagle, Double Eagle, Salmon-eaters, and other phratries began to display Beaver as one of their own crests. This signified their right to trade in pelts. Since trapping was their livelihood, it would not be proper for Beaver crest holders to claim they were descended from the animal. Who would kill their kinsfolk for a living? Instead, Beaver's crest was passed to humans for avenging a great wrong.

Beaver's Appearance
Beaver is identified by its prominent front teeth and a paddle-shaped tail. Never located on the back of the pole, the tail is folded upward in front of the body. Tails are textured with crosshatching or other markings. Beaver sometimes holds a stick or an arrow in the horizontal position in its front paws or in its mouth. The race of Giant Beavers with enormous tails is well known to humans. Some have extra animated faces on their tails and paws. When they die, the faces die with them.

Beaver Personality and Habits
Like their ordinary animal counterparts, Beavers are active, build dams and lodges, and raise their young. A race of Giant Beavers lives in communities with powerful chiefs,

speaks their own tongue or human languages, and composes their own songs. They are very deliberate in constructing huge dams, diverting rivers, and digging tunnels. They are cunning in their ways and clean in their habits. Unlike Bears, they are reclusive and care little about humans or their insults, except in one instance. They are short tempered if humans question their craftsmanship, engineering skills, or weapon-making abilities.

Beaver Powers

Like other animals, Beaver can appear as an ordinary creature or it can remove its skin and temporarily take on a human form. Giant Beavers are a race of beings with tails so large, one slap can start an earthquake or cause a lake storm. In certain circumstances, they can slap their tails and become invisible. Beavers keep their own supplies of sharp arrows and spears on hand should they ever be attacked. They use their teeth to sharpen these weapons and employ fine crafting techniques not generally recognized by humans.

Beaver's Relationship with Humans

In general, Beavers rarely fraternize with humans, preferring to keep to themselves. When humans invade their territory, they commit frightening acts, even to the point of murder, thus warning humans to keep their distance. To discourage human habitation, Beavers have been known to tunnel under a human vil-

lage. No one suspects their undermining until the ground collapses. In one case only, a human kept Beaver as a pet. In the presence of all humans except for its owner, it assumed the size and habits of an ordinary beaver. The

man became so fascinated with its alternate form that he neglected his own family. This caused jealousy among his relatives.

Hidden between the lines of the following story are hints about the rivalries between clans. The underlying story is about who has legitimate rights to use the "new" Beaver crest. Within the double meanings concealed in all native stories is the story of wars between competing humans. Read the story first as it is written and then read it a second time substituting "a rival group to the Beaver clan" for the word "Beaver."

Birds

Beaked birds from several species appear prominently on totem poles. These include Eagles, Woodpeckers, Hawks, Owls, Ravens, and several powerful mythological birds. The highest in rank is the Thunderbird.

The Eagle plays an esteemed role within many Native groups. All North American aboriginals use eagle feathers and down for ceremonial costumes, headdresses, and decorations. Mimetic Eagle dances echoing the raptor's soaring flight, wing movements, pinched looks, and dis-

Thunderbird over Whale

appearance into the clouds are performed everywhere in the world. Eagles are noted for their longevity, swiftness, keen vision, and the dizzying heights to which they soar. The Bald Eagle, for example, is the national emblem of the United States.

Thunderbird is an extremely powerful Eagle. A very old conceptual form appearing both in Asia and among various tribes of North American Native people, the image of a "bird that thunders" is prevalent from the Northwest Coast to California and as far south

A Composite of Beaver Stories

IN THE TIME BEFORE this, a household slave was ordered to awaken the chief, who did not arise at his usual hour. The chief's body was covered with a mat, an arrow was sticking out, and the man was dead. Nobody in the village knew how it happened or for what reason. The nephews of the chief extracted the arrow and saw that it was expertly crafted. They passed it round. Usually someone could identify an arrow by its markings, but this shaft was unknown.

After the funeral and rights of succession, a great feast was prepared. Everyone from far and wide was invited to come. In this way, the nephews hoped to gather information about their uncle's murder. Many people examined the shaft, but their information was of little use. One guessed that the Beavers had made it, but this suggestion was met with catcalls and insults. It was laughingly agreed that Beavers are awkward, and stupid, and they could not possibly possess the skill to create such a fine weapon.

One of the guests, a stranger wearing a beaverskin garment, took particular interest in the general derision. When the murder weapon was again passed round, the stranger spoke in a quiet voice, "This finely crafted arrow belongs to my brother."

At this pronouncement, the unknown man pulled his garment up over his head, slapped something hard on the floor and disappeared —taking the arrow with him.

Immediately recognizing the creature as Beaver, the feasters gave chase. As they neared the pond, they saw two huge Beavers sunning themselves. One had an arrow in its teeth, but both creatures quickly dived into the safety of their lodge. The villagers now agreed it was Beaver who had killed their chief.

The people prepared for war. (These rituals form part of the story, but they are not related here.) Gathering up shovels and using poles as levers and stakes, they burst the Beaver dam.

There are several versions of the battle that followed. Some say the Beavers were slaughtered on the spot; others say it took time until the Beavers came to inspect the damage. During the wait, as guards kept watch, the Beavers ambushed and killed some of the humans. Some say the Beaver wives managed to escape into a secret whirlpool.

All the stories agree on two vital points. First, one Beaver was covered with living human faces. As he died, all of its faces died with him. And the Beaver-Chief was so powerful, it took several men to subdue him. The spears of the Eagle clan struck true, but the spear of another warrior broke. Since the Eagles actually killed Beaver, they claimed full rights to use its crest; had the spear of the other not broken, that clan too would have had right. However, in the heat of battle, one spear faltered. That was a fact.

After the war, the chief and council decided to move their people to a more secure location. Beavers are powerful beings and their revenge can be severe. The stories diverge on the number of villages, their locations, and relocations. The villagers split up and resettled some distance away.

Many years passed and there seems to have been a continuing struggle over who was entitled to display Beaver's crest. Then one day, in one of the villages, a great clap of noise rumbled through the earth. When the people ran in panic, they fell into collapsing pits. Many were killed. Unknown to the inhabitants, the Beavers had undermined their village with hundreds of tunnels. The collapsing ground triggered nearby landslides that blocked the salmon run. A great famine followed.

Near another resettled village, the Beavers dammed a river, diverting the salmon. Another famine, another battle followed.

The stories go on to explain how the Eagle phratry used this period of famine and the subsequent disintegration of the social order to gain undisputed control over its use of the Beaver crest.

as Central and South America. Powerful Thunderbird also appears among Plains and Eastern Woodlands tribes. To many outsiders, Thunderbird is central to the concept of a totem pole. However popular its image may be, Thunderbird is not mandatory.

There are several other equally important beaked creatures who also appear as heraldic crests or characters in stories. Thunderbird's closest relatives and companions include Kolus, Hok Hok, Hawk, and Eagle.

Beaked Birds' Appearance
Thunderbird has an eagle-like beak, talons, claws, feathers, and raptor-like eyes. In previous times, Thunderbird always sported curly antenna-like ear bobs, while Eagle had no ears.

Today, carvers create Thunderbird figures without antenna or distinguishing ear pieces.

Kolus (also spelled Kulus, Quolus, Q'olus) is the younger brother of Thunderbird and its kin. Covered with dazzling white fluffy down, he sometimes becomes overheated—especially when he visits swampy, humid areas. He used

A Modern Thunderbird Story

IN THE TIME BEFORE this, a giant Whale the size of a mountain came to inhabit the oceans offshore. Its appetite was enormous, and each time it was hungry, great storms arose. The seas were swept clean of all life. The salmon did not return to the rivers and humans began to starve. One of the great chiefs climbed a cliff overlooking the ocean and begged Whale to leave. Whale ignored him. Still Whale fed and there was no food for humans. After a time, a council was called. Chiefs from far and wide tried to decide on a course of action. Leaving aside their personal arguments, they climbed the cliff. Though they used their best abilities, no matter how they begged, Whale ignored them.

Finally rituals were performed to invoke a greater power. (These rituals form a part of the story, but they are not related here.) No one would dare call on Thunderbird directly by name. Weeks went on, the famine deepened. One afternoon, black storm clouds swept in from the ocean. An invisible presence was felt among the people and a voice echoing with a thousand swirling winds demanded to know why it was summoned. When they made their request known, the presence was quiet. Finally it asked, "What will you do for me?" The chiefs consulted among themselves. Perhaps they could hold a series of potlatches in its honour? But they had been starving for many seasons, there was no food, and the people were depressed. A potlatch some time hence might not be the best compensation when the threat needed immediate attention.

Finally, one of the lesser chiefs had a bold idea. They would adopt a crest, authorize rights, and build totem poles in honour of this presence. Its image would appear above all others, on top of every pole in the land for all time.

The presence was pleased, and in a terrifying fury, it made itself visible. The awesome form of Thunderbird materialized from out of the storm clouds, lightning flashing from its eyes and talons, ear-shattering thunder rolling from under its wings. Thunderbird flew over the inlet and snatched up Whale in a single swoop. Stories diverge as to the ending of Whale. Some say Thunderbird ate Whale as usual; others say Thunderbird dropped Whale and it turned into a mountain still visible near present-day Duncan, BC.

Whatever the ending, Native people have kept their word. Thunderbird is seen topping many a totem pole among all cultures and many nations. And Whale is often seen, head down, right beneath.

Kolus is the square-headed brother of Thunderbird

Gull are rare depictions. Mosquito has a beak-like proboscis and is not a bird at all.

Beaked Birds' Personalities and Habits

Each beaked creature has supernatural strength, great dignity, and noble character. Thunderbird, Kolus, Hok Hok, Hawk, and Eagle are the royal family of the skies. Living in comfort, somewhere in the sky, with the usual complement of slaves, little is known about their personal life. Thunderbird does have a wife. The Natives of Siberia speak of female Thunderbirds who fly into a rage when humans ridicule the nakedness of their legs. Thunderbirds and their kind speak in several tongues, read human thoughts, and hold ceremonies of their own. They engage in wars with forces beyond the scope of human knowledge.

When Thunderbirds are in an area, lightning flashes and thunderclaps follow. Occasionally, human foibles annoy them and it is whispered that a Thunderbird, in a fit of rage, once tore a human to bits. Humans consider it expedient to invoke them only when necessary.

Thunderbird is sometimes sighted swooping down on a whale and lifting it aloft. This is its prey, which is consumed with great gusto high on top of mountains. Remains of whale bones found in the mountains are evidence of a Thunderbird's kill. Occasionally, it takes several Thunderbirds to lift particularly enormous whales.

Thunderbird has one archenemy. A ferocious horned underwater sea snake called

to sport ear tufts too, but they are often squared off today.

Hok Hok (also spelled Hokw-hokw or Huxwhukw), is also known as Koskimo, Khenkho, Crooked Beak of Heaven, or Cannibal Bird. Hok Hok features an enormously elongated beak. Hok Hok is really a form of Raven and features prominently in Kwakiutl Hamatsa dances. One of three cannibal birds, Hok Hok is an agent of the cannibal who lives at the north end of the woods. Its beak is useful for cracking skulls and sucking out eyes. It

is one of the cannibals that escaped the purge when the transformer rid the world of these creatures.

Unrelated birds (and beaked nonbirds) occupy a separate position in the hierarchy of totem characters. Owls are associated with the dead and darkness, while White Owl is a family crest along the Skeena River. Raven has a heavier looking beak than his raptor cousins and is part of a separate cycle of stories (discussed later in the chapter). Loon, Heron, and

Siskiutl (SISK-yu-til) almost matches its heavenly foe in power and cunning. Siskiutl also has the ability to change size and transform itself into a giant Woodworm. Thunderbird uses lightning to rip open trees in order to search for this manifestation of its enemy. The image of a huge eagle figure clutching a snake-like creature in its talons is prevalent in many cultures all the way to South America.

Kolus, the younger brother of Thunderbird, has a lot to prove. Noted for lifting heavier loads than its older brothers, it has been known to help humans raise their heavy bighouse beams into position.

Eagle is the equivalent of an earl or a lord, reigning among his fellow birds, but in status, a little closer to humans. As a bird of warning, it often plays a helpful role and has been known to rescue people about to fall off cliffs. In its viler persona, it steals babies. Occasionally groups of Eagles will get together and attack a whale, lifting it out of the water, just as their cousins the Thunderbirds do. Closely associated with Thunderbird, Eagle possesses many of the same traits.

The Hawk figure is much like its Eagle cousin, but more prone to taking on human form for long periods of time. During these periods it is known as Hawk-man or Hawk-woman. Known to interact freely with humans, Hawk also likes to eat mosquitoes—and mosquitoes are intimately

Basic Shapes

Split U

U design

Totem pole art contains characteristic shapes which give it a unique look among all other aboriginal art. By observing design details, one can see several unique shapes: the ovoid, the elongated U, and the split U, along with elongated shapes and circles.

Nested Ovoids

"Ovoid" is a unique term for a flattened oval shape that is intermingled, woven, and repeated in all Northwest Coast art. It sometimes appears on its own and sometimes is nested (as shown here) with additional ovoids or other shapes. With more squared corners than

Nested Ovoids

regular ovals, the term "ovoid" was coined about 1965.

Incised U

The U with a somewhat flattened bottom is also typical of the native art of the region. These forms are found in every possible orientation; right side up, upside down, and sideways.

The slightly off-centre orientation is a feel the Native artist brings to the work.

The Split U form is a variation of the regular U, and variable design mechanisms serve to divide the wide space between the two arms of the U. Split U's are common and are found in every orientation in Northwest Coast art. This particular split U, has a design flair on the bottom left corner, which is not present on all split U's.

These basic forms—the ovoid, plain U, and split-U—are part of the "alphabet", so to speak, of totem pole art.

linked to cannibal figures.

Hok Hok is a powerful bird, much concerned with its position as the central figure in a frightening human initiation ceremony called the *hamatsa*. A vital part of cannibal dances, Hok Hok oversees young human initiates sent into the rainy woods to starve. Returning weeks later to the warm longhouse, the initiates dance menacingly, threatening to eat the spectators. No matter what foods they are offered, they express a desire for human flesh. Hok Hok can crack open human skulls with its powerful beak. It enjoys brains as well as eyeballs. Its "hap! hap!" cry strikes fear into human hearts. It is good friends with Dzunkwa and Bookwus, well-known cannibals. Hok Hok is a manifestation of a flesh-eating Raven.

Raven and Mosquito are characters in separate stories, discussed later in this chapter.

Beaked Bird's Powers

All sky creatures can remove their feather cloaks, becoming invisible or assuming a human form. Thunderbird can readily read human minds. Best known however, is Thunderbird's ability to cause thunder and lightning. Various tribes offer different explanations. According to Tlingit stories, Thunderbird simply rustles its wings. The Haida say that lightning is caused by silver fishes hidden among its feathers or, in other cases, by a fiery dart sent forth from its mouth to kill whales. The Kwakiutl say lightning originates from the twinkling of Thunderbird's powerful eyes and thunder from its flapping wings, or thunder is the sound of dead ancestors echoing in its wake. The Nootka people offer several explanations. Thunder is its voice and lightning flashes from its talons; light-

ning is the glint in its eye; its neck is a snake that breaks free and scatters into lightning bolts.

Beaked Birds' Relationship with Humans

These powerful creatures live in an unknown dimension high in the sky. While they have the ability to read human thoughts, like all aristocrats they are mostly concerned with their own affairs. They intervene only when approached by an important delegation or a high-ranking person who observes the correct procedures. Occasionally, they have been known to transform and come down as humans to enjoy Winter Dance celebrations. A few fortunate humans have benefited from their intervention during house construction. Beaked birds are excellent at lifting heavy roof beams into place. Like all immortals, they can easily grant wishes—if they choose. It is sometimes dangerous to invoke them when they are involved in their own disputes.

Though Kolus is the raptor most likely to lift house beams, some humans insist it is actually Thunderbird. Any group fortunate enough to receive their help has the right to display their crests. At times, these magnificent raptors will warn their own heraldic crest people of an impending death.

Hawk Woman

Dzunkwa Tales

THE FOLLOWING Dzunkwa tale is a traditional account of Dzunkwa's powers and is not suitable for children. Besides the disturbing aspects of cannibalism, there are underlying themes of implied seduction.

In the time before this, the children of the village were playing outdoors. Clever Boy was by the side of the river when he discovered a log, so he and three companions floated away. After coming ashore, they were travelling deep into a dark forest when they suddenly noticed multicoloured smoke rising from a branch-covered hut. (The original story explains the symbolism of each colour within the smoke, but that is not related here.) No one was home, so they played with the interesting toys strewn about.

Suddenly, they heard a noise. A giant Dzunkwa was approaching, pursing her lips, cooing seductively, and offering the children a piece of red gum. Clever Boy was wary, but the other three were greedy. "Give us some gum," they demanded.

"Come," she said, "I will get you some." Collecting them up in her wide open arms, she placed them in her basket and took them to her hut. Sticking a piece of gum on the children's eyes, she knocked them out and went to bed. In one version of the story, her victims were slightly injured; Dzunkwa then took a stick, rubbed it along their wounds, and gave it to her own children to suck.

The next day Dzunkwa awoke and began preparing for a great feast. She chopped wood, made a fire, heated boiling stones, and prepared bentwood boxes for cooking. Outside her house, she removed layers of hemlock branches covering a long cooking trench. This she began to fill with hot coals. (The dances, songs, and rituals she performs form part of the story, but they are not related here.)

In some stories, Mouse-woman next told the children about their predicament. In others, they were well aware. The children knew they must escape. In various stories, there are different escape scenes. Only one version is related here.

Clever Boy was sitting with his companions hunched on the floor in one corner of the hut. He called his companions together and they conceived a plan. Clever Boy began fiddling with a toy bow. He shot a toy arrow out the doorway. Telling his sister to fetch it, the young girl sauntered out the door. Once outside, she ran homeward as fast as she could. Casually, Clever Boy picked up another arrow and shot it through the door. His younger brother, then the third child, casually repeated the girl's actions. Just as Clever Boy was about to repeat his ploy and pretend to fetch his own toy arrow, dull-witted Dzunkwa looked around and became very suspicious.

Quickly, Clever Boy devised an alternate plan. "Can I help you fetch some water?" he asked. Yawning widely, looking tired and very confused, Dzunkwa handed him a large container.

As he was stepping outside the door, Dzunkwa suddenly realized her folly. Running outside, she screamed to Bookwus, who was just arriving to join in the feast. "Our good dinner has run away," Dzunkwa explained. Hearing this, Clever Boy quickly climbed a tree and hid.

Bookwus, the Wild-Man-of-the-Woods, set off after the trio. (In the original stories, an involved "magical flight" scene ensued, but that is not related here.) The three escapees

72

dropped ordinary objects that turned into massive obstacles (for example a handful of pine needles became a thick forest) and temporarily delayed their pursuer. Coming at last to their own village, the children met a search party of warriors who arrived just in time to capture Wild-Man.

Meanwhile, deep in the forest, Dzunkwa was searching for Clever Boy. Though he was well hidden, she spied his reflection in a mirror-like pond. Looking up, she called seductively to him, "How is it you look so handsome?"

"I always put my head between two stones," he quickly replied.

"Then I will do so too," she said. "Come down and show me." So that she too can become handsome, the boy instructed her to fetch two heavy stones. On her return, she dropped them down. "Now, come and show me," she cooed.

Though it is not explained as such in the stories, it seems that in the act of fetching the stones, dim-witted Dzunkwa actually became caught up with the idea of becoming beautiful. The boy cautiously ventured down the tree.

"Now lie down," he said. The boy placed her head on one stone and told her to shut her eyes. He lifted the other stone and smashed it down as hard as he could. Her brains scattered everywhere.

Clever Boy quickly raced homeward. Meeting the search party, they combed the forest, found her hut, and heard the immortal Dzunkwa singing happily. The party of warriors set upon her. She and her companion were placed on mock-thrones and treated roughly. The village people discovered the glowing coal pit and finished preparing the very fires in which the creatures had planned to cook their children. With the flames leaping high, the warriors disposed of the giants. Cutting them into tiny pieces, they carefully dropped all the bits into the fiery pit. To make sure no single trace of the cannibals remained, the fires were stoked for four days and nights. Sparks and embers flew up, high into the skies, day and night, night and day. Little by little, overhead, a transformation occurred. The sparks turned, one by one, into swarms of buzzing, angry mosquitoes.

This explains why little mosquito is eager to taste your blood. And this explains why a squashed mosquito leaves little trails of gray "ashes".

Mosquito

73

A Composite of Mountain Goat Stories

IN THE TIME before this, the Mountain Goats were very angry because humans had been slaughtering them in large numbers. Many were killed for sport, not food; some were maimed for the fun of it.

One day some playful children caught a baby Kid down by the river. Imitating their elders, they made a fire and tried to burn it alive. Raven-Feather took pity on the little creature, rescued it, and kept the Goat hidden in his lodge. To heal its wounds, he rubbed a little fat on its burns and spread a little crimson salve around its eyes. When its strength returned, Raven-Feather took it back to its home in the mountains.

One day two strangers appeared in the village. Entering the chief's bighouse, they invited the whole village to a great feast. Everyone got ready, then followed the visitors up the mountain. When they came to a large mountain lodge, there was a sumptuous feast lying in wait. In one of the stories, the elders ignored their own children's warnings that their hosts were eating grass.

Without much appreciation for the feast, the villagers greedily gobbled up the delicious food. Some stories say they further in-

sulted their hosts by pilfering left-over food morsels and hiding them in their blankets.

While the guests were waiting for the after-dinner dances to begin, Raven-Feather observed the preparations. He noted that all the dancers wore goat-skin robes and mountain goat headdresses, and that they danced in an unusual way. One dancer had red circles around his eyes. In one story, this particular dancer approached Raven-Feather and instructed him to sit tightly against the wall; Raven-Feather quietly obeyed. In another story, the little boy was asked to sit at the place of honour. (The ensuing dances

and songs form a part of the story, but they are not related here.)

The leader of all the dancers had larger and blacker feet than the others. Unexpectedly, in the middle of one dance, he charged past the guests, jumped over the fire, and kicked a hole in the wall of the house. With all the tumultuous songs and loud drumming, the guests began to laugh. Once again, the black-footed dancer jumped over the fire, charged out through the hole, and kicked against a nearby cliff. As the guests continued to laugh, the big-house began to shake, a landslide was released, and the whole mountain began to collapse. The dancers calmly resumed their normal forms and scrambled agilely down the rock face. All the guests were killed.

In the morning, Raven-Feather awoke in the middle of a landslide. A Mountain Goat with painted eye rings stood watch and tenderly reassured him, "Because you saved me, I also saved you."

In certain stories, the boy returned to his village to discover he has actually been away for 10 years. The new people living in the village accepted him warmly.

Cannibals and Mosquitoes

Anthropophagy arouses emotions that are very powerful. That it was long ago practised on the Northwest Coast is beyond dispute. Dzunkwa (also known as Tsonoqoa or Tsonokwa and in previous times called Black Tamanous), is the figure most associated with the practice. Occasionally, she was joined in her ravenous pursuits by several like-minded companions: Bookwus, a short-beaked man-eating Raven, and snapping Hok Hok bird. These four players with taste for human flesh strike fear into human hearts.

Several southwest native, Inuit, Siberian, and Russian mythologies depict a "giantess" or "witch" with a basket or cauldron who carries off children. The Dzunkwa story related here is part of a worldwide cycle of stories embedded in many cultures. In folktales such as *Hansel and Gretel, Jack the Giant-Killer, Baba Yaga, Odysseus and Cyclops, Tantalus and Pelops, Van den Machandelboom,* and *Die Kinder in Hungersnot* stories the hero outwits a dull-witted ogre that eats human flesh. There are similar stories in India, Africa, and southern Australia. Certainly not meant to be a children's story, the Dzunkwa tale previous is a traditional account of this cannibal-kidnapper's powers.

Today, Northwest Coast Natives believe that cannibals left the earth a long time ago. However, among the Kwakiutl of Vancouver Island, dance simulations imitative of the practice continue to be performed each year. The flesh-eating creatures are believed to be monsters left over from the time when the Transformer rid the world of offending beings. Dzunkwa and her companions somehow escaped the purge.

Totem pole heraldic figures themselves were long ago linked with complex rules about who and what can and cannot be eaten. For example, Bear clan members usually cannot eat Bear, their kin. These taboos may stem back to earlier times and earlier practices.

The linking of cannibalism, Mosquito, and fire shows a keen appreciation for the annoying habits of the tiny blood-drawing insect. This link is shared with Romanian stories, where one tale says mosquitoes were created from the devil's pipe, and with a number of Filipino stories about mosquitoes carrying fire and becoming fireflies.

Dzunkwa's Appearance

Dzunkwa is a dark-skinned, human-like creature usually portrayed with round eyes, furry eyebrows (if present), pursed lips, and pendulous, drooping breasts. In recent times, political correctness has edited the breasts. Skin glowing in the dark, her hair (if present) fans out in all directions. Dzunkwas are numerous, but live solitary lives deep in the forest, on the outskirts of most Native communities. Also known as the Wild-Woman-of-the-Woods, her male counterpart is Bookwus, also known as Wild-Man-of-the-Woods, Pugmis, or Woodman. He exhibits many of the same qualities as his female companion but lives in an invisible house and attracts the ghostly spirits of the drowned to him. The pursed lips of both figures represent a kissing motion meant to attract little children with a "come hither" gesture reminiscent of calling a dog. Dzunkwa some-

Haida-style

Coast Salish-style

SINCE THE ART OF totem pole carving was revived in the 1950s, the personal style of individual artists has begun to dominate totem pole design. Today, Reid poles, Tait poles, or Cranmer poles display artistic forms characteristic of their makers. In turn, these artist-designers may or may not pay tribute to their own tribal origins.

Increasingly, modern totem poles are an amalgam of several tribal styles representing the best of several traditions overlain with the style of the designer.

In earlier times, during the Golden Age of Totem Poles, from 1830 to 1895, each band developed a characteristic style and individual carvers adhered strictly to it. There was little room for individual imprinting. The following descriptions represent ideals of traditional tribal styles and are only glimpsed in bits and pieces on modern totem poles. Today, there are many variations since totem pole carving primarily becomes a general expression of native pride, rather than a tribal-related form of expression.

Kwakiutl-style traditional poles are noted for brightly paint-ed colours of white, red, green, yellow, brown and black. Heads are large and blank eyes stare straight ahead. Unlike other poles carved in one piece from a single log, Kwakiutl poles feature add-on bits such as sun rays, whale fins, wings, or beaks. Figures are rigid and stiff. Winged Thunderbird dominates the top of almost all Kwakiutl totem poles. This figure has greatly influenced the totem pole movement everywhere. Miniatures, souvenir poles, and totem pole drawings feature the characteristic open-winged, rigid, straight-staring Thunderbird, first made famous by the Kwakiutl people.

Kwakiutl figures represent supernatural beings, with frightening overtones, known to live hidden inside their houses or nearby in the forest. Traditional and modern Kwakiutl poles are narrative in nature—that is, they tell a story and illustrate it.

Modern Kwakiutl poles are somewhat more relaxed, the eyes have greater depth and the overall pole is not completely painted. Thunderbird remains perched firmly on top.

Tsimshian-style poles made by traditional people along the Skeena and Nass Rivers contain two unique features sometimes imitated by modern artists. The poles are typically unpainted and come in a variety of forms (not all forms are illustrated here). The Pole is unlikely to feature a pole-topping Thunderbird, and the dominating bird, if any, is usually a long-beaked woodpecker or a curved-bill hawk.

Several, but not all, traditional Tsimshian poles feature bands of small people compressed between larger animals. The largeness of the mythical figures dominates the smallness of clustered humans and represents human inferiority to the divine. Each figure exhibits a separate personality with the exception of the humans, who are almost identical. The horizontal bands and variations in scale are said to stop the viewer's eyes from wandering and concentrate attention on the meaning of each layer. Totem eyes peer out in various directions, and there is less rigidity in the carvings than the strict discipline apparent in traditional Kwakiutl poles.

A second unique feature of some of Tsimshian poles is their simplicity. Certain poles (not shown here) are no more than a long unornamented shaft surmounted by one three-dimensional animal. This type of pole provides a contrast to the heavily ornamented surrounding poles and serves to elevate the eye up to the crowning figure. An example of this type of pole is shown on page 19.

Traditional Tsimshian poles are largely monuments erected by various families to commemorate their chiefs after death. They correspond roughly to tombstones. Scholars surmise that it was the Tsimshian peoples along the Nass and Skeena Rivers who

Nuxälk-style

Kwakiutl-style

Tsimshian-style

created the first clusters of free-standing totem poles.

Haida-style poles reflect their people, who were a seafaring lot and regularly visited their neighbours to the north and south. This and their excellence in the arts explains the wide influence that the Haida style continues to exert on the totem pole traditions of the Northwest Coast. Shown here is a tall Haida pole cut into three pieces to illustrate the characteristic "eye set" of the figures. Far from a vacant stare, Haida eyes are designed to peer down at the viewer from their position on the pole. Well-formed eyes feature inner pupils and outer lids, pinched on two sides. The figures peer down in eternal watchfulness. The higher the figure on the pole, the more angled downward its gaze. Haida poles are typically unpainted and feature voluptuously carved semi-human and animal figures. The lines of Haida poles flow from one decoration to the next. Humans, if they appear at all, are smaller than other figures. Some feature a thrusting tongue. Thun-

derbird does not feature in their depictions. All Haida poles show fully dimensioned animals, with well-rounded body parts and separate personalities.

In times past, Haida poles were mainly monuments erected by various families to commemorate important people after death or to commemorate the happenings at a potlatch.

Coast Salish–style poles were uncommon. The Coast Salish people and their cousins to the south traditionally did not build totem poles or create multitudes of different masks. While many band members have adapted to new ways and now build impressive freestanding poles, the characteristic carvings of these people were single figures. These wooden human figures adorned graves or stood along the shoreline to attract the attention of their seafaring neighbours. Today, called greet figures or welcome figures, the traditions behind these slightly-larger-than-life-sized "poles" go further back than the carving of regular tall totem poles. Coast Salish people today do carve de-

tached totem poles. Some appear to be a number of greet figures, one on top of the next; others look like an amalgam of several tribal and artistic styles.

Nuxälk-style pole art is not well known and exerts a minor influence on modern traditions. Isolated in a deep mountain valley, the Nuxälk (Bella Coola) people once had few visitors and thus developed their own unique style. Relative latecomers to the art of totem pole construction, Nuxälk poles feature well defined and separated shapes such as teardrop, triangle, and leaf shapes, slightly uncharacteristic of other Northwest Coast traditions. The poles are brightly painted and have few add-ons. Eyes stare straight ahead and contain a contrasting coloured pupil.

Today, the Nuxälk are renowned in artistic circles for depicting the round-faced figure of Siskiutl in a deep blue colour to match the skies and ocean of their homeland. Their execution of this creature surpasses that of all other traditions. A Nuxälk Siskiutl is pictured on page 87.

times carries a basket to capture small children. As a masked dance figure, Dzunkwa holds her hands palm out in front of her mouth and eyes, in order to hide her true intents. In certain stories, it is said her hands are sharp as knives. On public totem poles she sometimes stands, arms open, attracting hoards of unsuspecting tourists into her wide embrace.

Mosquito has a long proboscis and is sometimes mistaken for a bird. But his crafty eyes give his true tastes away. He is a story figure, not a heraldic crest.

Dzunkwa's Personality and Habits

Dzunkwa is an uncivilized, brutish woman who lives in the forest. Suffering from some sort of sleeping (or drug-induced) disorder, she sleeps much. Her eyes are slit-like, and even when awake she is trance-like in her movements. In her active periods, she prowls the edge of villages attempting to satisfy her appetite for children's flesh. Sometimes she has to settle for stealing fish. Her house is made from fir branches, and when awake she gathers roots, flowers, herbs, and resins from which she concocts a tasty gum-confection to attract children and glue their eyes shut. Always saccharin in her approach, her true intents are murderous.

In recent times, political correctness has unfortunately edited her pendulous breasts and her personality. In one case she was recently described by a major museum as a "loving mother embracing the world." Dzunkwa would be pleased. She has several chil-

The Goodwill Pole

"GOODWILL" HAS MANY shades of meaning but rarely rises to the ironic levels of the Goodwill Pole. In 1899, a Goodwill Mission travelled to Tongass, Alaska, to "help" the natives. During their stay, the visitors pilfered a pole and removed it to Seattle. The villagers immediately sent representatives south to protest—to no avail. In 1941, as part of the first serious efforts to preserve US totem poles, descendants of the Tongass villagers were employed to restore the totem pole in Pioneer Square. As a gesture of "goodwill," they officially presented it to the city of Seattle.

Ainu Poles

THE AINU, the aboriginal people of northern Japan's Hokkaido island, also carve poles. Ainu mythology tells of a people closely connected to water. Pole groupings such as these represent the "Playground of the Gods" and tell the story of supernatural beings who came to earth to give birth to them. Bear, Owl, and Orca are particularly significant figures for they are the earthly disguises the gods assume. Ainu pole groupings are designed to complement the background scenery. Each pole is simply made and it is the sum

of the grouping that creates the effect.

Frog is associated with granting wealth

dren of her own. What exact psychological problems they exhibit are not fully explored. Since they are taboo, she does not eat them. In fact, she is deeply upset when they are injured, maimed, killed, or spirited away and put on display. She makes heroic efforts to resurrect them. The attack on her children is unrelenting. Anyone who can make her babies cry can demand her treasures. These include a magic canoe, water of life, or death-bringer (handy if you are really angry at someone). Compassionate humans, who help her get her children back, are showered with gifts.

Bookwus, on the other hand, engages in slightly fewer forays for human prey and prefers to fraternize with frightening ghosts.

Dzunkwa's Powers
Significant among Dzunkwa's power is her ability to resurrect herself from the dead. Even with her brains smashed out and her body dismembered,

she can reassemble and come alive. She also can use this power with her own children, who have frequently been murdered to spite her. If she can get their bodies back, she can rouse them from the dead.

Dzunkwa's Relationship with Humans
Sometimes, Dzunkwa leaves her home in the forest and visits humans during their Winter Dances. When inside the longhouse, a human attendant ropes her around the waist with a leash. Because she is permanently dazed and in some sort of hypnotic state, unless she has help, she cannot circle the fire four times before she falls in. Those fortunate enough to come across Dzunkwa's home while she is away come back with dried meats, skins, statues, and coppers. She enjoys a lively side-practice of thievery and has been known to pilfer a hunter's or fisher's entire catch. Her greatest interest in humans, however, is dietary.

Frog
Frog is the heraldic crest of several active clan lineages that exist to the present day. In Western cultures, Frog usually belongs to the beast-marriage cycle as in *The Frog Prince*, or *Frog Went a-Courting*. Along the Northwest Coast, Frog never appears in marriage sagas; Instead, Frog plays a peripheral role in stories and in one tale (not related here), each time a frog is sighted, a voice cries out for the return of a beloved daughter who has died.

The qualities admired in Frog are its abilities to survive red hot volcanic lava flows or scorching fires, to live on land or in water with equal aplomb, and to burrow deep in mud yet continue to breathe. Frog has several alternate personas and in those forms is associated with bringing copper and wealth up to the surface from underwater cities.

Frog's Appearance
Very realistic in interpretation, Frogs appear top to bottom, or bottom to top, hidden in other figures' ears, on top of their heads, or embedded in their belly buttons. In each case, Frog represents the Frog clan's association with the pole.

Frog's Personality and Habits
Little is related about Frog except for its usual shift-shaping qualities and its occasional transformation relationship with Copper Woman and Woman of Fire.

Frog's Powers
In one story, Frogs are associated with calling humans who come back from apparent death, but exactly what power

Frog brings to bear on this process is not quite clear. In another story, Frog is held down in a fire with a stick and when it bursts, a lava flow engulfs the village. Copper Woman, Frog's transformed self, associate, or alter ego, is noted for bringing wealth. She is the wife of Komokwa, or Copper Maker, a powerful guardian of the undersea world. Woman of Fire, Frog's second persona, is noted for her destructive tendencies.

Frog's Relationship with Humans

Frogs are generally unconcerned about humans and in many instances are treated with contempt. In one story, a fisher and his companions prepare their catch over an evening campfire. From out of the darkness, a Frog leaps out and pushes their dinner into the flames. The vexed humans kill the creature and begin to cook their dinner over again. A larger Frog, with bright copper eyes, hops out and repeats the action. The angry humans burn it. The third time, a larger-than-life Woman appears in a pillar of flame. In her hand, she carries a talking stick mounted with a copper Frog. She tells the fisher that he and his companions will die. After many other story incidents, related one by one, all happens as foretold.

Human Forms and Human Objects

Coppers are shield-shaped devices that played an important role during a potlatch. On totem poles, a copper often means that the owner of the pole is displaying a heraldic animal or figure for the first time.

Frog is the heraldic crest of the Frog clan

The right or prerogative to carve an animal or heraldic figure was granted to the pole's owner in one of three ways:

    (a) at a potlatch
    (b) through war
    (c) through an encounter with a supernatural figure

    To show that the new prerogative is approved , the new animal or figure holds a copper. A Bear with copper appears on page 35.

Chiefs

Chiefs are recognized by their three-ringed hats. Each time an elder was able to mount a pot-

A Frog Story

IN THE TIME before this, a great man climbed a high mountain to learn what he could from Mountain-Spirit. While on top, he had a vision. A Giant Frog came and told him that humans and frogs were part of the one-ness of all. Humans should treat Frog with more respect. When the man came out of his trance and returned to his people, they took Frog as their emblem and built totem crests in honour of Frog.

Crying Woman

Humans

Humans clustered in horizontal bands on Tsimshian poles represent the lesser role of helpless humans as contrasted with the superior powers of transforming animals and mythological beings. On modern poles, it has become fashionable to show humans joining hands to illustrate a spirit of cooperation among all of humanity.

White people, such as the man in a top hat crowning the famous Abraham Lincoln pole in Alaska, represent the coming of Europeans to liberate or dominate native cultures. The Lincoln figure, now kept indoors at a museum in Juneau, Alaska, was erected in Tongas village about 1870 to proclaim that President Abraham Lincoln had liberated Native American people as well as southern slaves.

Mountain Goat

Mountain Goat is part of the cycle of stories about redressing the imbalance caused by hunters. It is also a heraldic crest. A fairly rare depiction on totem poles, its heraldic variations are Painted Mountain Goat and Mountain Goat of Skedans. The Raven phratry has rights to display Mountain Goat.

Mountain Goat's Appearance

With one or two prominent horns and hoofed feet, Mountain Goat is occasionally mistaken for some sort of a devil depiction. This is not the case. Its hooves and horns simply reflect its natural ungulate form.

latch, he was entitled to weave another ring on top of his cedar-strip hat. Three seems to be the maximum number shown on poles, although hats with up to seven rings are displayed in some museums. A chief's presence on a pole usually means he commissioned the totem pole. His carvers have wisely chosen to feature the image of their benefactor among the heraldic crests and story figures.

Clusters of three chiefs represent the Haida Watchmen, an ancient society entrusted with guarding Haida Gwaii, the ancestral home of the Haida nation

Crying Woman

Crying Woman is a story figure, not a heraldic crest, on several poles. In each of her appearances, she is crying for a different reason. On one famous pole near the Skeena river, she is crying because she has captured a grouse to save her starving son, but she is too late.

Whale appears beside one head of Siskiutl. Thunderbird conquers another Whale behind.

crest related to this practice is the powerful Sea Wolf or Wasco image; some say it is not Wolf at all but a powerful Grizzly-Bear-of-the-Sea. Wasco (in Wolf form) hunts whales and lives in a mountain lake near Skidegate.

A whale carcass or two usually floated ashore each year and its meat was greatly savoured by the tribes that did not venture onto the open seas to hunt whales. It is said that because a cedar-made Whale figure once carried out the wishes of a starving human, whale fat crackles in the fire just like wood.

Whale's Appearance

Two species of whales can be distinguished on totem poles: Gray Whales and Killer Whales. Their body parts are sometimes rearranged with the tail, major fins, and head appearing in a somewhat detached fashion, fitting as necessary around the pole. On several poles, the dorsal fin is attached as a separate piece and thus is subject to falling off. Whale is usually carved head down, and on many totem poles happy faces peak out from the blow hole. There is no significance to these happy figures; Native carvers simply like to fill spaces with interesting designs.

Whale's Personality and Habits

Whale is generally seen as prey so its personality and habits, powers, and relationship with humans, like Salmon, are less defined than some of the greater entities. It is difficult to include likable personalities on the menu. In the Thunderbird story, one particularly obnoxious giant Whale plays a major role as the antagonist. In other

an arrow. Whale then went to live, with many personified sea creatures, in an underwater city. This act of kindness granted the descendants of the injured person the right to use Whale's crest.

Since ancient times, harpooning whales at the climax of fortnight-long seagoing voyages was the activity of the Nootka people. Because of the dangers involved, great ceremonies verging on shamanism were part of the practice. Whaling team members were initi-

left: Wolf

ated, underwent fasts, were ritually prepared, watched special dances, and enjoyed rights greater than ordinary individuals. Whale as a totem figure on some poles descends from the rights of whalers and whaling.

Among the Kwakiutl and others, it was said that Whale came ashore after a long time at sea, plowed up on the land, and changed into Wolf. In that shape, it enjoyed hunting land animals and occasionally its own kind. In Wolf form, it revealed the secrets of the Whale cult to all humans. The Haida

IN THE TIME BEFORE this, there was a great famine upon the land. Now the people were starving. Their discomfort was heightened night after night as they listened to the beating of drums and loud howling songs coming from across the river. The people were afraid to go out, even in daylight.

One brave warrior volunteered to investigate. Venturing forth in his ceremonial robes, his face painted, his long hair tied in a knot, and armed with weapons, he ventured out. (These rituals form a part of the story, but they are not related here.)

Crossing the river he came upon a huge Wolf, whining in agony. As the warrior approached, it laid back its ears and gazed at the intruder, begging with pathetic eyes. "Come brother, what has happened?" the warrior inquired. Wolf could not speak, but opened its mouth in a cavernous yawn. Sizing up the situation, the warrior approached. Behold, a deer bone was stuck in Wolf's throat.

With reassuring words, the warrior removed the bone and Wolf immediately recovered. Joyously, it licked the warrior's hands and feet. Then emitting a loud howl, it disappeared into the forest.

The next day there was a tumultuous howling from across the river and the people could see scores of Wolves pacing restlessly on the opposite shore. The warrior and his companions were once again summoned. While the party was crossing the river, the Wolves disappeared. Arranged along the opposite bank lay sev-

eral deer carcasses. There was great rejoicing among the hungry people. Each day more deer carcasses appeared, along with mink, martin, and groundhog to be distributed as gifts. The warrior and his people were able to mount great feasts. By the prerogative of this event, all these people adopted the Wolf crest. It is said by some that the warrior himself was made Prince-of-the-Wolves.

The story goes on to explain how their association with Wolf permitted them to obtain magical headdresses and robes from the Ghost-People. (These rituals may form a significant part of the story, but they are not related here.)

Sometime after, strife broke out and there were disputes over who had abused certain privileges associated with the masks taken from the Ghost-People. In the end, the warrior and his immediate family left their tribe and went to a new area to found a new Wolf phratry. Other branches of Wolf clan use the heralds Tall Conical Hat, Long Sharp Nose, Hanging Across Half Man, and Sea-Wolf. Wolf phratries once claimed the rights to the tallest poles along the Nass River.

stories, Whales are well known to be the prey of Thunderbird and Eagle.

Wolf

Wolf has a varied reputation throughout the world. Its faithfulness to its family and strong group loyalties have done little to prevent it being maligned by many societies. Being associated with evil, it was hunted to extinction in much of Europe.

Among North American native people, Wolf exhibits a nobler personality. Wolf and Raven, or Wolf and Beaver are moiety divisions of the Tlingit people. Wolf is also prominent in the heraldic imagery of Coast Salish, Quileute, and Makah (southern Nootka) peoples.

Some of the first "human" Wolf phratries claim blood relationship to the animal. It seems four cubs survived a great flood by climbing to the top of a tall mountain. There, they removed their clothing and became human. Eventually, their offspring wondered if they were the only people in the world. Putting on Wolf masks, they howled aloud. Finally their cries were met with an answer. They left the mountain and went to live among ordinary humans. There are several variations of this story. Other Wolf clan origin stories are taken from the cycle of "grateful animal" tales.

Wolf's Appearance

Wolves have long muzzles with sharp teeth, but usually not the sharp incisor teeth of Bear. Bear also has a shorter muzzle and more rounded nostrils. Wolf's ears are pointed. Wolf can be integrated on a pole from top to bottom or in full body sitting on its haunches. The tail is sometimes present and sometimes not. In recent depictions, Wolf looks quite realistic.

Wolf's Personality and Habits

Wolves live in remotely located communities, in enormous bighouses, and have all the normal feelings associated with families toward their brothers, sisters, children, and spouses. Stories do not say whether they keep slaves. Deer are their favourite prey. Though Wolves know the secrets of hunting and curing sickness, they are little inclined to share either with humans.

Wolf's Powers

Taking on the form of humans and speaking in human tongues are basic animal powers. In the case of Wolf though, transformational powers sometimes occur in reverse. Certain humans not only become like Wolf, they become Wolf.

Wolf packs host elaborate late-night dance celebrations noted for loud drumming, howling songs, and beautiful women. During these ceremonials, Wolves transform into lively human-looking dancers and are known to fraternize with long-dead Ghost-People. Occasionally, humans have crept unnoticed into these ceremonies, only realizing their folly when they play a trick on a female dancer: trying to reach up a dancer's skirts, they feel nothing but the bare bones of death.

Wolf will sometimes travel to the ocean and change into Whale. This is why both wolves and killer whales hunt in packs.

Wolf's Relationship with Humans

Mostly wary of human encounters, Wolf nevertheless retains the ability to commit to friendships and render helpful services to people. According to some, a Wolf (transformed from Whale) once revealed the secrets of hunting Whale. Usually, however, Wolves show a vague lack of interest in human affairs, preferring the camaraderie of their own kind. One Wolf society originated when a great shaman killed a Wolf chief and danced in his skin, thereby gaining the power to cure all ailments. Wolf society members know many secrets; certain members can even become Wolf. This society will enact the Wolf dance for a sick person, but the charge for such a cure is very high.

Traditional Cedar Products

THESE ARE SOME traditional cedar products made by the First Nations people:
- large canoes
- nets, traps, weirs, and harpoons to harvest salmon
- watertight bentwood boxes for cooking
- storage boxes
- large plankhouses to house up to 50 families
- cedar bark mats used for many purposes
- baskets for berry picking and food storage
- cedar burial boxes
- woven clothing and waterproof rain hats
- feast dishes
- totem poles and sculptures

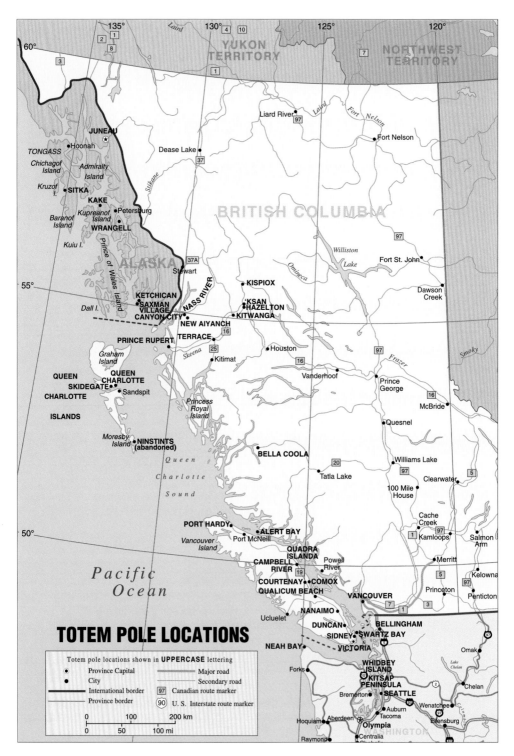

TOTEM POLE LOCATIONS

Totem pole locations shown in **UPPERCASE** lettering

- ● Province Capital
- ● City
- International border
- Province border

- Major road
- Secondary road
- 97 Canadian route marker
- 90 U.S. Interstate route marker

| 0 | 100 | 200 km |
| 0 | 50 | 100 mi |

4. Land of the Totem Poles

Ever watchful eye

This chapter locates authentic, well-designed totem poles and totem pole collections from Seattle, Washington northward along the Pacific coast of British Columbia to Juneau, Alaska. Some of these totem poles have official names and some do not. The names listed here are descriptive only.

Alert Bay: Vancouver Island
Alert Bay is famous as the Kwakiutl village that defiantly continued its practice of the potlatch at a time when it was illegal to do so.
• Collection of Poles—Restricted Nimpkish Cemetery
• World's 2nd Tallest Totem—Near U'mista Centre

Bella Coola
Bella Coola is an isolated village accessible along a difficult gravel road or by water. While there, it is advisable to request that an escort accompany you to view an area of rare petroglyphs.
• Small Collection and old Longhouse—Village centre

Bellingham: Washington
• Outdoor poles—Whatcom Museum of History and Art

Campbell River and Quadra Island: Vancouver Island
In and around Campbell River is the heart of Kwakiutl country—famous for the immortal Thunderbird topping almost every pole. Quadra Island is a ten minute ferry ride from Campbell River.
• Big Man with Copper Pole—1400 We-Wai-Kum Road

- Cemetery Poles—Reserve, Band Cemetery
- Dzunkwa Pole—Tyee Plaza Shopping Centre lot
- House posts, Thunderbirds—Foreshore Park
- Kaysoo Crest Pole—Kwagiulth Museum, Quadra
- Two Poles—Coast Discovery Inn
- Thunderbird Pole—New Campbell River Museum
- Welcome Figure—Kwagiulth Museum, Quadra

Duncan: Vancouver Island

A walking tour map is available from the Cowichan Valley Museum on Canada Avenue and Station Street, Duncan, BC. Painted yellow footsteps lead the way to all 39 totem poles.

- Collection of Totems—Museum, Canada Ave & Station
- Collection of Totems—Walking Tour of Duncan
- Native Heritage Centre—Near Duncan Bridge
- Rick Hansen Memorial Pole—Museum grounds, Canada Ave
- World's Thickest Totem—Station Street and Jubilee

Haida Gwaii
(the Queen Charlotte Islands)

The totem poles at Ninstints and Tanu are only accessible by boat or sea-plane. Tourists must leave each of these areas by nightfall. The Queen Charlotte Islands require a seven hour ferry crossing from Prince Rupert.

- Bill Reid Pole—Skidegate Band Office
- Davidson Poles—Old Masset
- Decaying Poles 1—Ninstints (by water)
- Decaying Poles 2—Tanu (by water)

In June of 1791 at Ninstints on Anthony Island, near the southern tip of the Haida Gwaii (Queen Charlotte Islands) a notorious atrocity occurred. American sea captain John Kendrick suffered the loss of his personal laundry from aboard his ship and responded (as was the naval custom of the day) by seizing a Haida chief and his companion. He ordered his crew to bolt their legs in a gun carriage, until the pilfered laundry was returned. To the proud chief Hoya, this was a grave insult.

Revenge was planned. When Kendrick and his men came ashore two weeks later, Hoya and his people swarmed aboard and commandeered his ship. Kendrick stalled, then delivered a counterattack killing more than 50 Haida people. Hoya himself was wounded.

Strong-arm tactics such as these, were not forgotten. As late as 1878, a Haida shaman's party, encountering Canadian researcher George Dawson, demanded to know if he was a "Boston" man. On being reassured by numerous references to British royalty, they left the research party alone.

Today, Ninstints, more properly called the village of Skungwaii, is an abandoned village in ruins. The remains of decaying totems loom in the frequents mists. Longhouses, shell middens, and more than two dozen totem poles, some at various angles, speak of a people who departed long ago. Abandoned since the smallpox epidemic of 1861, the site is teeming with nearby colonies of puffins, petrels, seals, and seabirds. Accessible only by water, many tour companies offer day trips into the area. The heritage site is under the administration of the Haida Gwaii Watchmen, a traditional society who have protected their island home for thousands of years.

Juneau, Alaska

Juneau, the gateway to Glacier Bay, has several totem poles and shelters a large brown bear and bald eagle population in the area.
- Centennial Poles—Centennial Hall, Egan Drive
- Century-old Totem—State Office Building
- Collection of Old Totems—Alaska State Museum
- Famous Lincoln Pole—Juneau Museum
- Two Poles—Auk Tribe Building

Kake, Alaska

The third tallest totem at 150 feet high is located here along with a collection of other totem poles.
- World's 3rd Tallest Totem—Kake

Ketchican, Alaska

According the U.S. National Record, Ketchican boasts the world's largest collection of original, old totem poles.
- Collection of Poles—Saxman Native Village
- Collection of Poles—Totem Bight Historical Site
- Collection of Poles—Totem Heritage Center
- Old Poles—Tongass Historical Museum

Kitsap Peninsula, Washington

- Chief's memorial—Suquamish Museum

'Ksan and Native Villages: Northwest British Columbia

Within a 50 kilometer radius of the reconstructed traditional native village of 'Ksan near New Hazelton BC, stand several collections of totem poles within Gitksan native villages.
- Bighouses and Poles—'Ksan Indian Village
- Collection of Poles 1—Gitsegukla
- Collection of Poles 2—Gitwangak
- Collection of Poles and Fort—Kitwanga
- Collection of Poles 3—Kitwancool
- Collection of Poles 4—Hazelton
- Totem poles and Hatchery—Kispiox
- United Pole—Kispiox Band Office

Nass River Poles: North of Terrace

Most of the original Nass river poles were harvested by anthropologists during the collecting frenzy a century ago. A few new poles are being erected.

- Tait Sunbear Pole—Canyon City/Gitwinsihlkw
- Unity Rainbowman pole—School yard, New Aiyanch

Neah Bay: Washington

- Artifacts and Remants—Makah Cultural and Research Center

Prince Rupert: Northwest British Columbia

One of the "city totem pole" collections, dozens of these totems were harvested and brought here in the 1920s and 1930s. However, not everyone appreciated their value—at first. When one pole tipped over during a weekend windstorm, concerned citizens were hard pressed to find its pieces. The following week, it was discovered in a public building, in the furnace room, neatly chopped up for firewood. It was rescued and later replicated.

- Collection of Poles—City Tour Map available
- Gitlakdamix Pole Replica—Museum, McBride and 1st Ave
- Haida Beaver Pole—Museum, McBride and 1st Ave

Route of the Totems: British Columbia

As part of the revival of totem pole building that was underway during the 1960s, the province of British Columbia commissioned 11 carvers to build 19 poles which were placed along the tourist route from Victoria to Prince Rupert. The poles are each about four meters in height and are built around the unifying theme of "Bear". The most important poles, outside the major cities along the route are listed in order from south to north, starting near Victoria, Vancouver Island. The balance of the "Route of the Totem" poles are listed under the appropriate city listing.

- Bear with Frog—Sidney Ferry Terminal
- Grizzly Bear of the Sea—Swartz Bay Ferry Terminal
- City with 39 Totem Poles—Duncan, BC
- Eagle with Bear—Pearson Bridge, Nanaimo
- Thunderbird with Bear—Ferry Terminal, Nanaimo
- Golden Eagle with Bear—Qualicum Beach, Island Highway

- Kolus Pole—Infocentre, Courtenay
- Twin Poles—Lewis Park, Courtenay
- Hok Hok with Sun and Chief—Comox Reserve, Bighouse
- Grizzly Bear with Salmon—Port Hardy Ferry Terminal

Seattle, Washington

In addition to the Goodwill Pole at Pioneer Square, there are a number of well carved poles scattered around Seattle.

- Artifacts and Poles—Thomas Burke Memorial Washington State Museum, U of Washington
- Chief John Wallace's Pole—MonHake Cut on E.Shelby Street
- Duane Pasco Collection—Occidental Square
- Goodwill Pole and others—Pioneer Square
- Poles and Feasting—Blake Island
- Seattle Center Pole—Corner of Center House
- Traditional Poles—North of Pike Place Market

Sitka, Alaska

With prevalent reminders of its Russian occupation, Sitka also features authentic totem poles and a cultural center. Some of the oldest intact poles in the world are found here.

- Collection of 28 totem poles—Sitka National Historical Park

Terrace and Kitsumkulum, Northwest British Columbia

The native community of Kitsumkulum is only a few kilometers from Terrace. Since most of the original poles in the area were harvested in the great museum collecting frenzy about 100 years ago, these are poles are about a decade old.

- Diamond Jubilee Pole—3205 Eby Street
- Two Poles—Highway 16 near Terrace

Vancouver and Area: Lower Mainland

One of the finest totem collections in the world is found at the Museum of Anthropology, 6393 NW Marine Drive. There is also a small simulated native village outdoors on the grounds.

- Bear Mother Poles—VanDusen Gardens, 37th & Oak
- Centennial 100' Pole—Maritime Museum, Cypress St.

- Coast Salish Housepost—2525 West Mall, UBC Campus
- Collection of Totems 1—Stanley Park
- Collection of Totems 2—UBC Museum of Anthropology
- Dzunkwa Pole—CBC Bldg., 700 Hamilton Street
- Expo '86 poles—Plaza, 750 Pacific Blvd.
- Hunt Pole & Carved Doors—Horseshoe Bay Park, W. Vancouver
- Japanese Ainu Poles—Burnaby Mountain Park
- Tait Pole, outdoors—NEC, 285 E.5th Avenue
- Tait Poles, indoors—Capilano Mall, N. Vancouver
- Three Watchmen Pole —Border Crossing, Blaine, WA
- Weeping Woman Pole—VCC, 100 West 49th Avenue
- Whale Pole—2136 West Mall, UBC Campus

Victoria: Vancouver Island

The Royal British Columbia Museum features a well-researched collection of poles outside the museum and a comprehensive collection of artifacts and old totem pieces inside.
- Bear with Copper—Government Street & Belleville
- Collection of Poles—Thunderbird Park, Douglas Street
- First Men Tall Pole—Beacon Hill Park
- Hunt Family Crest Pole—Royal BC Museum courtyard
- New-style Salmon Pole—Saanich Commonwealth Place
- Three Watchmen Pole—Royal BC Museum entrance
- World's Tallest Totem—West over the Blue Bridge, turn left

Whidbey Island, Washington
- Haida Raiding Totem—Deception Pass State Park

Wrangell, Alaska

The poles at Wrangell are not located in an easy-access tourist area; please check access.
- Collection of Poles—Kiks'adi TotemPark

Reference

Recommended Reading

Barbeau, Marius. *Totem Poles.* Ottawa: Queens Printer, 1950.

Brown, Jospeh Epes. *The Spiritual Legacy of the American Indian.* New York: Crossroad Publishing Company, 1982

Drew, Leslie & Douglas Wilson. *Argillite, Art of the Haida.* Surrey, BC: Hancock House, 1980.

Efrat, Barbara S. and W.J. Langois. *Captain Cook and the Spanish Explorers on the Coast.* Victoria, B.C.: Sound Heritage, Queens Printer, 1978.

——. *The History and Survival of Nootkan Culture.* Victoria, B.C.: Sound Heritage, Queens Printer, 1978.

Feest, Christian. *Native Arts of North America.* London: Thames and Hudson, 1992.

Gill, Sam D. & Irene F. Sullivan. *Dictionary of Native American Mythology.* New York: Oxford University Press, 1992.

Goodchild, Peter. *Raven Tales: Traditional Stories of Native Peoples.* Chicago: Chicago Review Press, 1991.

Gunther, Erna. *Art in the Life of Northwest Coast Indians.* Portland: Portland Art Museum, 1966.

Hawthorne, Audrey. *Kwakiutl Art.* Seattle: University of Washington Press; Vancouver: Douglas & McIntrye, 1988.

Holm, Bill. *Northwest Coast Indian Art: An Analysis of Form.* Seattle: University of Washington Press; Vancouver: Douglas & McIntrye, 1965.

——, *Spirit and Ancestor.* Douglas and McIntyre, Vancouver, 1987.

Jonaitis, Aldona, ed. *Chiefly Feasts, the Enduring Kwakiutl Potlatch.* Seattle: University of Washington Press; Vancouver: Douglas & McIntyre, 1991.

——. *Art of the Northern Tlingit.* Seattle: University of Washington Press, 1986.

Kew, Della, and P.E. Goddard. *Indian Art and Culture.* Vancouver: Hancock House, 1974.

MacDonald, George F. and John J. Cove. *Tsimshian Narratives 1.* Collected by Marius Barbeau and William Beynon, Canadian Museum of Civilization, Mercury Series. Ottawa, 1987.

——. *Tsimshian Narratives 2.* Collected by Marius Barbeau and William Beynon, Canadian Museum of Civilization, Mercury Series. Ottawa, 1987.

Macnair, Peter L. *The Legacy.* Vancouver: Douglas and McIntyre, 1984.

Maud, Ralph. *A Guide to B.C. Indian Myth and Legend.* Vancouver: Talonbooks, 1982.

Nuytten, Phil. *The Totem Carvers: Charlie James, Ellen Neel and Mungo Martin.* Panorama Publications, 1982.

Sommer, Robin Langley. *Native American Art.* London: Bison Group, 1994.

Stewart, Hilary. *Looking at Indian Art of the Northwest Coast.* Vancouver: Douglas and McIntyre, 1979.

——. *Looking at Totem Poles.* Vancouver: Douglas and McIntyre, 1993.

University of British Columbia. Museum of Anthropology. *Northwest Coast Indian Artifacts.* Vancouver: University of British Columbia, 1975.

Wallas, James, and Pamela Whitaker. *Kwakiutl Legends.* Surrey, BC: Hancock House, 1989.

Wardell, Allen. *Objects of Bright Pride*, 1978.

Index

The Author

"No matter how often my native friends explain particular poles to me and no matter how many academics write well-researched papers, totem poles still have a certain undefinable 'something' about them that defies explanation." says Pat Kramer, author.

Kramer first worked for native people during a graduate research project in Alberta. Long since a transplant to the British Columbia coast, she now instructs tourism courses at the Native Education Centre. There she values the friendship of her students who are learning to start their own tourism ventures. When she is not busy teaching, she is on the road attending festivities, visiting native communities, and taking the photographs that appear in these books. She also travels to various archives and libraries to do the research that allows readers to cover complex subjects quickly. Each summer she conducts several special interest tours. Ranging through the ancient cliff cities of Arizona, searching for therapeutic hot springs muds, or attending powwows, Kramer's clients are always impressed with the aboriginal wonders of North

Pat Kramer

America. Now in her second term as President of the Western Tour Directors Association of Canada, she is part of an industry team setting certification procedures for tour directors in western Canada. In addition to several student publications, Pat's other books are: *B.C. for Free and Almost Free*, (Whitecap Books); *Native Sites in Western Canada* in English and *Indianer in West-Kanada* in German (Altitude Publishing), and *Quickguide to Northwest Coast Native Art* (Remark Publishing).